Ontario's Vanished Villages

FORKS. OF. CREDIT
ONT

Ontario's Vanished Villages

Ron Brown

Polar Bear Press
Toronto

This book is dedicated to my Mom who, over my life, has probably been more patient with me than I ever deserve.

Polar Bear Press

distributed by
North 49 Books, 35 Prince Andrew Place, Toronto, Ontario M3C 2H2
(416) 449-4000

Canadian Cataloguing in Publication Data

Brown, Ron, 1945-
        Ontario's Vanished Villages

Rev. ed.
Previously published under title: Vanished Villages
Includes bibliographical references and index
ISBN 1-896757-11-1

1. Ghost towns — Ontario — History. 2. Ghost towns - Ontario - Guidebooks.
3. Historic sites — Ontario. 4. Historic sites — Ontario — Guidebooks
5. Ontario - History, Local.   I. Title   II. Title: Vanished Villages

FC 3061.B79 1999   971.3   C99-930254--X
F1058.B79 1999

00 01 02   10 9 8 7 6 5 4 3 2

Table of Contents

Introduction

This is the story of a vanishing heritage. It is one that tells how Canadians in Ontario found their dreams stripped away by forces that they could not control nor could often understand. It is about the fur traders in the remote, drafty fur posts. It is about the first hardy pioneer settlers who risked it all to carve a home and a future from forests that for them held dangers of which they could not conceive. It is about the men and women who milled the wheat and cut the logs in Ontario's earliest mill towns, and the train crews who spent so much time away from home in the whistlestops and divisional towns. It is about those who toiled in the dark mine shafts, and who guided schooners into the tiny lake ports, and who hacked the ground in search of gold or silver, and who cleaved down the great pine forests. Most particularly, it is about the communities that they formed and the villages that they created; villages that exist no more. In a way they were all victims — victims of changing times and technologies. These changes often meant hardship and heartache for those forced to tear up their roots and leave behind their homes in the vanished villages of Ontario.

The most fascinating things that link us to our past are those physical, tangible things that say: "Here the old wood-burning locomotive stopped to load up; here the lumber baron drank his whiskey; here lived a community of 300 working men and their families." These are the old houses, town plots, manors, sleepy rail stations, abandoned mills and wrecks that still exist throughout Ontario.

Occasionally some effort is made to preserve what little is left but the power of urban development is often overwhelming, and much is being lost. The pages that follow capture the essence of this vanishing Ontario, to give you some idea of the world which is disappearing beneath the sprawling cities and towns.

The next time you cruise down a country road, give a moment's pause as you rush past that skeleton of a farmhouse, a silo left derelict, or the moss-covered headstones in some old, forgotten graveyard.

Ron Brown
March 1999

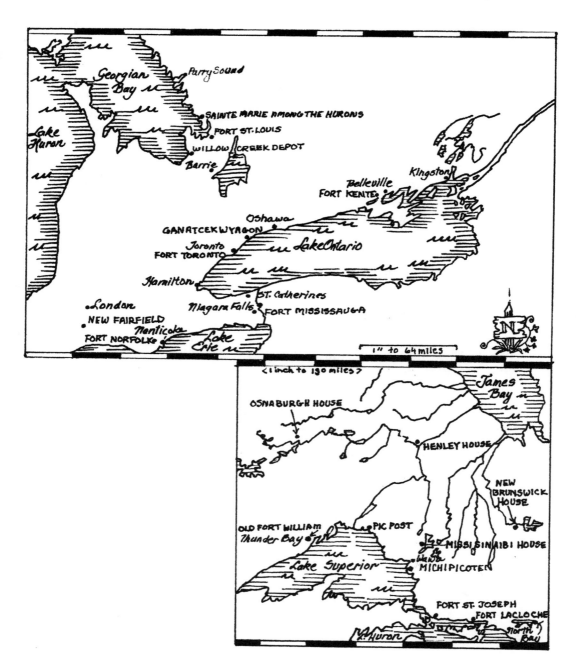

1

Fur Forts and Musket Balls

B efore the railways and even before the pioneer roads were hacked into dark forests, Ontario was quite a busy place. Native villages with their palisades and longhouses looked over fields of corn. And from these places the men would set out to check their trap lines and make their annual treks to the fur forts.

By the late 1600s Ontario had become a battleground between two rival fur companies: the Hudson Bay Company and the Northwest Company. At first the rivalry was simple. The HBC controlled the shore and the watersheds of Hudson Bay, while the NWC controlled pretty much everything south of that, including the Great Lakes watersheds. It was in that watery no man's land between the two where the competition grew fierce. The early NWC forts at Kaministiquia and Nipigon drew the native traders southward, while the HBC posts at Moose factory and Fort Albany drew them north. The NWC added others at Fort Charles (now part of Minnesota) and Fort St. Pierre (now Fort Frances) in the west and Temiskaming and Michipicoten in the east.

The HBC retaliated by moving inland and building posts of their own at Henley House, Gloucester House, Martin Falls, Osnaburgh, Frederick House and Brunswick. During the headiest days of the rivalry the two managed to build over 600 trading posts between them in Ontario. By 1821 the rivalry was too much and the two enemies amalgamated under the HBC. While many posts were closed, 125 of the larger ones remained open. By the late 1800s however, changes were happening that would nearly eliminate the fur trade. First of all, much of the game was being depleted. Then with the arrival of mines and the railways, the face of the north changed forever, and in all but 52 locations, the fur posts were abandoned. When the railways arrived, with the CPR in 1885, the Canadian Northern in 1912 and the National

HBC bunkhouse at Moose Factory is one of several fur trading buildings preserved in what is Ontario's oldest surviving non-native settlement.

Transcontinental a couple of years after that, the HBC moved all its fur operations to railside. Today even these are gone, except in few remote native settlements. Of most, little is left though they weren't much to begin with — a few log buildings in a forest clearing. The forest has reclaimed them today, and the sites offer little to see.

While the fur trade flourished in the north, settlers in the south were busy cutting their pioneer farms from the thick forests. But looming over their heads was the ever-present threat of raids from the restless Americans south of the border. It wasn't enough that they had beat the "bloody British" in the Revolutionary War, but they wanted more, of Canada, that is. To defend against the threat, the British built a string of forts. Many of the largest remain today, preserved as historic sites: Fort Erie, Fort Henry, Fort George, and Fort Wellington, all recreate the military era. Others, however, have vanished with little or no trace, and these are Ontario's ghost forts.

Fort Kente

Don't let the signs pointing to Fort Kente fool you. This 17th century Sulpician mission has long vanished, its exact location a mystery. It didn't last very long. Established in 1668 by missionaries, Fénelon and Trouvé, it was overshadowed in 1680 by the construction of Fort Frontenac at what is now Kingston, and was closed. The modern-day replica, however, is worth a visit as a way of revisiting the earliest days of European infiltration of Native Ontario.

Ganatcekwyagon

Now utterly overwhelmed by the Greater Toronto Area's suburban sprawl, this 17th century Iroquois village marks the site of Ontario's first school, built by Fénelon and Trouvé. Archaeologists estimate that the village, whose name means, "opening in the sand hills," lasted from 1650 to about 1700. It was this visit by the French priests that gave the place the name it has today, Frenchman's Bay.

Sainte Marie Among The Hurons

Canada's most famous reconstructed mission to the natives, Sainte Marie Among the Hurons was established by Jesuit missionaries in 1636. Following vicious raids by the Iroquois in the 1640s, nearly wiping out the Huron nation, the site was burned and abandoned. Eminent archaeologist Wilfred Jury began to excavate the site in the 1950s, and bit by bit it was reconstructed. Today it is a living museum operated by the Ontario Government, and retells the story of the Black Robes, as the Huron dubbed the missionaries, and the tragic and horrifying martyrdoms they suffered at the hands of the invading Iroquois. Inside the palisade are farm buildings, the chapel, the shops

Years of research produced this outstanding recreation of the ill-fated Jesuit mission, Sainte Marie Among the Hurons. There were similar missions in the area whose whereabouts remain a mystery. One was recently discovered and rescued from a gravel company.

11

of the various craftsmen, and accommodation for the priests. Separated from this enclosure was the area set aside for the native population that resided at the mission. All buildings are reconstructions, except for a few foundations that were part of the original complex.

Fort St. Louis

Only a cairn marks the spot now, a few kilometres south of Sainte Marie, but it was on this site that the invading Iroquois exacted their grisly vengeance upon the Jesuit martyrs Lalemont and Bréboef. The natives that survived the slaughter raced to Sainte Marie where they warned the others in time to escape.

New Fairfield

Most of those who didn't support the rebels during the American revolutionary war got out after the final shots were fired. A group of Delawares living in the Ohio Valley at a Moravian mission who had supported the British realized that they would have to move to Ontario, or face bitter reprisals by the victorious Americans. In 1793 they moved to the La Tranche River (now called the Thames) and built 38 houses and a church, and by 1800 had more than 300 acres under cultivation. But during the War of 1812, a vicious raiding party

An abandoned residence is one of only two buildings remaining in the Moravian Delaware community of New Fairfield.

12

led by American G.P. MacArthur swept up the Thames valley, destroying much of what was in its path. That included Fairfield. Following the attack they moved across to the south side of the river and rebuilt, calling their new home New Fairfield. While several families descended from the original group still occupy modern homes on this First Nations territory, a church and house from the early days of New Fairfield sit vacant on the south shore of the river.

Henley House
This was the first of the HBC's inland forts. Built in 1764 it stood on the Albany River eight miles from the forks of the Kenogami. The HBC built a large blockhouse to command both branches of the river. It was closed in 1857, and by the end of the century all traces had vanished.

Osnaburgh House
One of the most strategic of the HBC inland posts, this palisaded fur fort on Lake St. Joseph was built in 1786 and was home to up to two dozen men. In 1930 the site was flooded by the waters of a hydro dam at Rat Rapids, and the name shifted to present-day "Osnaburgh House", a First Nations community near Pickle Lake.

New Brunswick House
One of the HBC's most important fur routes was that along the Moose-Missinaibi River Valley. Moose Factory, one of the earliest and most important of the forts lay at the mouth of the Moose River on James Bay. Here were the trading post, fortifications, blacksmith and homes for the HBC traders. The other end of the route lay on Lake Superior at Michipicoten, where a former NWC post stood. In between stood New Brunswick House and its half dozen outposts. While the fur forts were more permanent, the outposts tended to be temporary and close to the native hunting grounds. The valley saw the first move of the HBC inland to compete more doggedly with the NWC. The NWC responded by building rival forts in almost the same locations. New Brunswick House was begun in 1788 and by 1821 could claim a two-storey master house, a barn, fish shed, a forge and five-foot stockade. After the 1821 amalgamation there was a new

rival — Americans based in Sault Ste. Marie. To counter this new threat the HBC embarked upon a policy of encouraging the natives to trap the animals to extermination near the Americans while practicing conservation measures further north near their own posts.

By 1825 the outposts and the rival NWC posts were gone and only New Brunswick remained, the sole post between Moose Factory and Michipicoten. Gradually the HBC abandoned the Missinaibi route and used Montreal instead of Moose Factory to ship furs. In 1872 New Brunswick House was abandoned.

Missinaibi House

Halfway between New Brunswick House and the post at Michipicoten stood Missinaibi House. When the Missinaibi River route was abandoned, Missinaibi House was better located than New Brunswick House for shipping furs to Montreal. The river was easier to travel and fur-bearing animals remained plentiful, while elsewhere they had been trapped to near extinction. All New Brunswick's functions were transferred there, and by the end of the century it was the most lucrative post in the district. The post consisted of the master's house, outbuildings, and cultivated land. Following 1885 when the CPR was built through the area, the post began to decline. Then in 1917, five years after the Canadian Northern Railway had laid its tracks through the northland, the HBC trading post moved to Peterbell on the railway. As recently as 1956 some of the buildings still stood, semi-collapsed log shells.

Natives gather at a Northern fur trading post.

Old Fort William

The grandest of the northern fur forts, Fort William was built by the NWC in 1807 to replace an earlier post on the Pigeon River (then in American territory). Within its huge palisade were the great hall, a stone munitions house, as well as bunks, barracks, shops and stores. It was the site of the annual "rendezvous" a great festi-

This early painting depicts Old Fort William as it originally looked when it hosted the annual rendezvous.

val at which the partners from Montreal would meet with the wintering partners. The site was on the shore of the Kaministiquia River where it flowed into Lake Superior. After 1821, when the HBC assumed the NWC operations, Fort William's functions were moved to Michipicoten, and the population at the fort dwindled. By the 1880s, when the CPR began to build its line west, only the stone munitions building remained. Then, when the CPR needed that land for its Fort William yards, down came the last vestige of the old fort. In the 1970s the Ontario Government reconstructed Old Fort William several miles upstream. Today the annual rendezvous lives once more, and the living museum recalls accurately the glory days of the fur trade.

Michipicoten

Originally an independent fort, owned and managed by Alexander Henry, it was purchased by the NWC, as were several other independent forts, and added to their network. Michipicoten was more strategic than most, marking as it did the gateway to the Missinaibi fur route, the most important of the North's fur highways. Its importance grew even more after 1821 when following amalgamation the HBC moved the functions of Old Fort William to Michipicoten. In 1877, at a cost of

The Michipicoten Post replaced Old Fort William in importance but shortsighted owners in the 1950s demolished the only remaining structure.

nearly $3000 (roughly, half-a-million dollars today), it was completely rebuilt and operated until 1904 when Great Lakes Power purchased the site. The main building survived until 1952 when Great Lakes, ignoring pleas from local citizens in Wawa to save the historic post, ordered it demolished. Today only a few cellar holes mark the location.

The Pic Post

A short distance northwest of the Michipicoten Post the Pic River flows into Lake Superior. Here on the flat, sandy shore stood a pair of early independent posts. Started by Gabriel Côté and a trader named St. Germaine, the posts consisted of master houses and warehouses. Bought first by the NWC, in 1821 they became part of the HBC empire and in 1850 were described as a group of whitewashed buildings with red trim grouped about a central square and surrounded by a palisade. Their location was also important as a convenient stopping place for voyageurs on their long canoe voyage from Nipigon to Michipicoten. After the CPR trains began rumbling along the Superior shore in 1885, the HBC removed to railside at Mobert. Both the site of the fur post, and that of the nearby port of South Heron Bay are empty now, active only when campers gather there in the summer.

Fort Lacloche

Here on the north channel of Lake Huron, Fort Lacloche began as a NWC post and was later absorbed by the HBC. It operated until near the end of the 19th century when the rails of the CPR arrived, and was abandoned. Situated at the mouth of the outlet of Lake La-Cloche, the ruins survive to this day on the grounds of a Ministry of Natural Resources ranger camp. Access is via a series of dirt roads that lead south from Massie.

Fort Toronto

Also known as Fort Rouille, Fort Toronto was a French fur fort built even before the establishment of the NWC or the HBC. With the victory of the British over the French in 1763, it was abandoned and later replaced with Fort York. The site is celebrated with a monument on the grounds of the Canadian National Exhibition.

Toronto

"Place of Meeting" in the Huron language. So named because it was the first stop on an overland shortcut between Lakes Ontario and Huron. Previously called the city of York by the British colonists, Toronto was renamed when the city was officially incorporated in 1834.

Fort Mississauga

The only missiles hurled at Fort Mississauga today are golf balls, for it sits abandoned right in the middle of the Niagara-on-the-Lake golf course. It was built in 1814 to complement the massive Fort St. George at Niagara-on-the-Lake, and reduce the threat of a repeat attack from the Americans. While the British garrison was housed at the latter, little Fort Mississauga stood directly across the Niagara River from the omnipresent threat posed by the American Fort Niagara. It was abandoned in 1870. Hostilities erupted again when, 100 years later, Parks Canada declared its plans to restore it. The golfers rebelled and the fort has remained a ruin.

Fort Norfolk

When, following the American Revolutionary War, the Yanks began to threaten Canada, Governor Simcoe set out to build more forts. The bluff above Turkey Point on Lake Erie seemed ideal to spot American ships and repel any landing. Beside it was the "bridgehead" village of Charlotteville. When the War of 1812 ended, both were abandoned and gradually disappeared. Abandoned forts seem to attract golf courses and Fort Norfolk was no exception. When the Turkey Point Golf Course was under construction old cannons were unearthed, but other than that, there is no trace of this once important fort.

Willow Creek Depot

The American threats meant that the Great Lakes had to be fortified and some of the most important garrisons were those at Fort St. Joseph and Michilimackinac on Lake Huron. The safest route to them was overland from Fort York, up the Humber River carrying place to Fort Gwillimbury (today's Holland Landing), and across Lake Simcoe to the head of Kempenfeldt Bay. From there they followed the Nine Mile Portage to Willow Creek Depot and down the Nottawasaga River to Georgian Bay. A hellishly swampy and malarial place, the depot consisted of a few leaky log buildings surrounded by a flimsy palisade. Eventually the portage was replaced by a road to the naval garrison at Penetanguishene, and the British troops gratefully abandoned the depot.

Though there was never any doubt that the military depot existed, by all accounts those forced to seek shelter there had wished that it hadn't. But was there ever a village at the depot? It's a question that has intrigued local historians for a number of years. While there are no historical accounts of one, not in any of the military diaries or in

The trenchworks are the only original features to survive at Willow Creek Depot.

any early travellers' accounts, later historians have argued that a pioneer settlement did exist. Writing in 1948, Andrew Hunter said "In consequence of the great amount of traffic quite a little village grew up at the northwestern terminus of the Willow Creek Portage". Robert Thom, an expert on Georgian Bay, has noted that CPR track layers dug up some graves, and speculated that the village existed sometime between 1816 and 1830. Excavations by Wilfred Jury, however, while showing the cellar holes of the depot along with the trail to it, found no archaelogical evidence that would support a village. Few now even mention the debate, and it is a question that will likely never be answered.

Located by the Minesing Swamp northwest of Barrie, recent attempts by the local conservation authority to reconstruct it met with vandalism, and today the only original traces are earth works and wagon ruts.

Fort St. Joseph

In 1783 the Treaty of Paris, which was signed after the American Revolution, forced the British to move their forts off American soil. Obliged to abandon Michilimackinac, they chose the nearby island of St. Joseph. Built in 1797 the fort consisted of a blockhouse, bake house and guardhouse, partially enclosed in a rickety, wooden palisade. So harsh were the conditions that when a NWC fur trading settlement grew up around it, many of the officers rented accommodations there rather than endure the misery of the drafty fort. When the War of 1812 broke out, the British commander at Fort St. Joseph rounded up several hundred militia and Indians and captured Michilimackinac. However, while he was there the Americans showed up at Fort St. Joe. Finding no one home, they burned it and then marched on Sault Ste. Marie which they burned as well. After the war the British returned Michilimackinac once more to the Americans, and abandoned St. Joe. In 1978 the federal government opened a visitor centre at the ruins of the fort. None of the buildings have been reconstructed and the site remains a picturesque ruin on the windswept waters of Lake Huron.

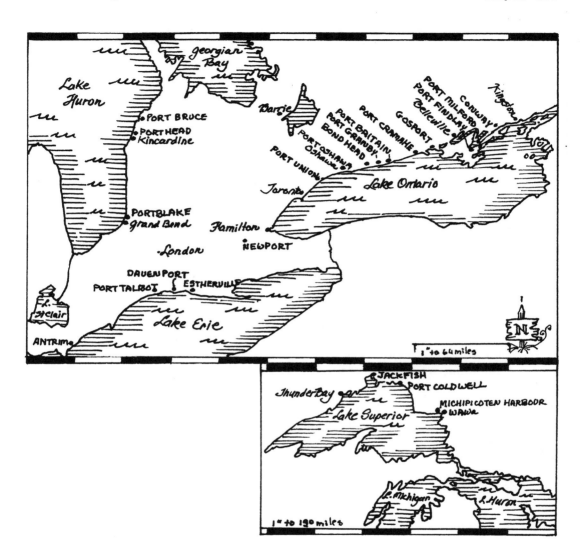

2

The Lost Lake Ports

Among Ontario's prettiest places are the little lake ports that snuggle in the coves and inlets of the Great Lakes. On Lake Erie there is Port Stanley where handsome 19th century buildings line the harbour, Port Dover where more than 40 squat, white tugs make it the home of the world's largest fresh water fishing fleet, Port Burwell with its ancient lighthouse, and on Ontario, the twin ports of Port Hope and Cobourg with their picture postcard main streets. These are all well known places and drawing cards for tourists. But among them are the lost ports of the Lower Great Lakes, places that thrived when the lakes were the only highway, when most shipping was by schooner to the American ports on the opposite shores, and when most roads were quagmires, and railways were unheard of.

The lands beyond the lakes are gentle and fertile. Rivers wind their way to the lakes creating at their mouths little coves where schooners could tie up to a small wharf and shelter from the winds. Here is where Ontario's first permanent villages appeared. In the early years there was little difference between them — wharves, warehouses, and piles of lumber and produce cluttered the shores, crude cabins housed a few fishermen, while brawling lumbermen and sailors tumbled out of the dock side taverns. Somewhere not too far upstream there was likely a sawmill or grist mill, while beyond the rough and tumble of the docks the stately homes of the proprietors stood discreetly behind lawns and trees.

The 1850s and '60s changed all this. By 1856 the Grand Trunk had built its main line connecting Toronto and Montreal. Those ports with larger harbours like Port Hope, and Cobourg boomed with the arrival of the steel rails. Meanwhile harbours that were too small for the steamers that the railway age demanded, withered and died.

Few have vanished completely. The attraction of living by the lake has simply been too irresistible and many of these once boisterous little ports are now quiet residential communities. Yet the ghosts are there. Old docks have tumbled into the waters, the warehouses have been replaced, usually by pleasant lakeside parks, and the taverns by newer homes. However, most retain some of the ghosts of the days when the forests stood dark and intimidating behind them and they were Ontario's only link with the world outside.

LAKE ERIE

Antrim

It's a name that doesn't even appear on maps anymore, but when traveller William Smith visited Antrim in 1846 he described it as "a small village on Lake Erie and the shipping Port for the surrounding neighbourhood with storehouses for storing produce for shipment, a tavern etc. [and where] vessels are occasionally built and repaired." The site is on Kent County Road 17, about 5 km from Morpeth.

Newport

Located not on the lake but well upstream on the long vanished Grand River Canal, Newport of the 1840s could claim a tavern, a store, and a pair of warehouses for storing the grain. 60 people called the place home. The Port along with the canal have vanished with little trace, although a one- time community centre and a couple of early houses still linger from farm days. It is a short distance south of Brantford.

Port Talbot

Despite the name, this was never a Port of any consequence. Rather it was the office from which Thomas Talbot haughtily handed out lands to settlers in the 29 Lake Erie townships which he administered until 1836.

Thomas Talbot was one of Ontario's most eccentric land promoters, and one of its most successful. By the young age of eleven, he had a commission in the British army (being born into wealth didn't hurt). From 1791 - 4 he served as personal secretary to Upper Canada governor John Graves Simcoe, giving him the opportunity to enter the land promotion business. In 1801 he moved to a point of land

Port Talbot was the location from which Colonel Thomas Talbot doled out land grants to settlers who passed his rigid standards.

overlooking Lake Erie, and there built his castle. From there he administered the most successful land settlement in southwestern Ontario. By 1836 he had settled more than 30,000 pioneers on land throughout 29 townships. His eccentricity earned him many enemies. If he didn't like the appearance or demeanor of the prospective settler, the unfortunate soul would get no land. Even for those who got land, Talbot refused ownership until they had satisfied all his conditions of clearing the land and erecting a house.

Estherville

Surrounded now by the busy town of Port Burwell, the site of Estherville is marked only by a Baptist cemetery. Between 1840 and 1890 it contained a store, hotel, church and shipyard. The lumber for the ships came from the forests that stood on the lands behind. But once the trees had been cleared the shipyard closed. Eventually the railway arrived at nearby Port Burwell, and Estherville faded, then disappeared.

Davenport

This was another Lake Erie Port that vanished when a more promising port boomed nearby. Its founder, wealthy English immigrant

Henry Dally envisioned a bustling port on the shores of the lake west of Catfish Creek. His project involved cutting a channel west from the creek where he had laid out a street and several lots. The site attracted a store, tailor, post office, a hotel and warehouses. In 1847 Daniel Hanvey pushed the government to help build a railway from London down to the shore of the lake. But the railway never arrived, and the channel was never cut. Meanwhile a little to the east, Lindley Moore had found a better harbour and went about promoting Port Bruce. The doomed little port-that-never-was sank into oblivion, and its residents moved their homes to Port Bruce. The old port is hard to even locate now as the road and many of the old town lots have since slipped into the tossing waters of Lake Erie.

LAKE ONTARIO

Port Granby

By the 1840s most of the forests that hovered over the shores of Lake Ontario had been cleared and in their place fields of grain waved gold-

A few ghosts yet lurk in old Port Granby although it is now a quiet residential com munity.

en in the breeze. There were no railways then and farmers sought out the closest place to ship their grain to market. Although the tiny harbour could only accommodate a few schooners, Port Granby soon contained three grain elevators, houses, store and March's Hotel. Contemporary directories list its population as being anywhere between 50 and 60. Its main exports included barley, 10,000 bushels a day at its peak, and pine from the Oak Ridges Moraine further inland. But improved roads allowed the exporters to use larger ports such as Port Hope, and Port Granby faded. In 1890 a Port Hope newspaper lamented that the once "growing village" was now "crumbling in ruins." Of the early buildings, only the hotel, now a residence, and the school have survived, along with a few houses. They lie along a gully on Lakeshore Road west of Port Hope.

Bond Head

William Smith passed this way too in 1846 and noted that Bond Head was having a rough time of it. This "village and shipping place contains about 50 or 60 houses which are very much scattered and about one third of which are occupied, no store open, one tavern open, two or three shut up". Despite the bleak picture on Bond Head's streets, the harbour remained active. The main exports that year were 70,000 feet of lumber, and 24,000 bushels of wheat. Things improved when a few years later the surveyors for the Grand Trunk Railway appeared and Bond Head's population jumped to 200 while land prices tripled. By then it had more hotels, a grist mill and grain elevator. But despite the arrival of the railway, the hated McKinley Tariff which restricted American trade with Canada, dealt a devastating blow to the shippers. A few years later a dam upstream broke and filled the harbour with silt. The mill was demolished in 1899, the elevators a few years after that.

Located south of Newcastle just east of Toronto, there are ghosts of the past yet at Bond Head. On the main street that leads into the village there are some fine examples of old houses and hotels while many of the old village streets remain empty. The site of the mill and elevators are now an attractive park while on the opposite shore a marina caters to modern mariners.

Conway

The old Bath Road today is being promoted as part of the "Loyalist Heritage Trail" and that would make the ghosts of Conway smile. The "Trail" follows modern roads through Prince Edward County and the shores of Lennox and Addington County that more or less cover an old pioneer route. Historic communities that line the route like Wellington, Picton and Adolphustown were all early Loyalist centres. Conway, south of Napanee, with its steamer dock was one of the busiest. Its deep water allowed larger steamers to call and gave it an advantage over the smaller schooner harbours. By 1865 it had a population listed at 800 with a hotel, stores and a number of small industries. But the railway passed several miles to the north, and stage and steamer service dwindled. By the turn of the century its population had plummeted to a scant 25, as its shops and industries fell silent.

The Oshawa Sydenham Museum has preserved three historic buildings from old Port Oshawa.

Port Oshawa

This site has probably the best preserved remains of a ghost lake port. Originally named Port Sydenham, Port Oshawa was the shipping point for the village of Oshawa several miles north. From the wharf went lumber and farm produce, while a mill was located about halfway between the port and the town. When the Grand Trunk Railway built its line through the area, shipping at the port declined. Today the Oshawa Sydenham museum has preserved three of the original Port Oshawa houses, the Guy House (1835), the Henry House (1849) and the Robinson house (1846). The Oshawa Archives is located here with brochures that describe walking tours of the many historical buildings that survive in this growing city.

Port Britain

Located just west of Port Hope on Lakeshore Road, Port Britain is an historic cluster of old houses that represent only a small portion of the once busy port. Before 1848 when the port was busiest, it exported 200 masts a year to the Royal Navy. It could boast a wagon maker, two coopers, two storekeepers, a tailor, a hotel, a grist mill a saw-mill a tannery and a carding mill, and 350 people. Plans were made to deepen the inner harbour and 100 lots were created for sale. When the

Grand Trunk Railway arrived in 1856 it built its tracks right along the lake where it established a station. But the depression of the day scuttled the plans for the harbour, and the town's expansion. Then, when portions of the track began tumbling into the lake, the GTR hastily rerouted them a mile further inland. Port Britain dwindled rapidly into what it is today, a small settlement of homes.

Today, by the intersection of Lakeshore and Port Britain Roads, a half dozen of the port's original buildings cluster: the hotel, the small house called Sora Brook (one of its earliest) and the beautiful stone house built for Robert Marsh, brother of the village founder, William.

Port Cramahe

This place hasn't succeeded in vanishing, for many early homes yet line its streets. However, its heyday as a busy port for the town of Colborne about a mile away has long since faded. During its life it underwent several name changes and was variously known as Colborne Harbour, Cat Hollow, and now Lakeport. A plaster mill, grist mill, sawmill, flour mill and distillery all provided cargo for the schooners that plied the lakes. Many of those ships were built right in the yards at Port Cramahe. Steamers also called, carrying passengers for Kingston, Toronto or Oswego. The ruins of the Keeler Grist Mill lie along the road to Colborne itself. Another dock further west, known as Grafton Harbour, was also a busy shipping point. By 1890, both had seen their last sailings.

Gosport

Important for shipping lumber and produce, Gosport also became a busy fishing port. From its three wharves in 1841 Gosport grew to become Lake Ontario's fifth largest fishing port. A grist mill operated a short distance up Butler Creek. But by 1920 it was declining and today has become one of the lake's lost ports. There is a marina, motel and various newer homes, however, only a couple of old buildings remain, both dating from the 1840s.

Port Milford

Somewhere in the waters off what used to be Port Milford lie the rot-

27

ting remains of the schooner Fleetwood. One dreadful night the ship turned from the channel toward the light that would guide it to the dock. The little craft suddenly shuddered and a sickening cracking sound reverberated through its timbers. Almost immediately the crew knew they had been lured by the phony lights of the pirates on shore. They weren't the only ones, for this was a ruse commonly practiced by pirates in the early days of Ontario's little lake ports. By the 1850s, the building of proper lighthouses, and the demise of the schooner ports drove the pirates out of business.

The docks at Port Milford were built by James and William Cooper, to which they added warehouses, a house and general store. Nearby, A. W. Minacker also had a store, hotel and wharves of his own. The end of shipping may have ended the wharves, but it didn't end activity at Port Milford. As Prince Edward County farmers turned to vegetable growing, the Church brothers opened a cannery at the site. This attracted a street full of workers' cabins. Finally when the cannery closed in the 1930s, Port Milford became a ghost town. While the house and old general store yet stand, only foundations mark the site of the cannery, and grassy mounds the workers' homes.

Port Union

With only a pair of dilapidated old buildings, one boarded, Port Union looks like a typical ghost town, and right in Scarborough. Located on the lake at the foot of Port Union Road, just south of Lawrence, its roots go back to the 1840s when local farmers, frustrated at the lack of a port from which to ship their grain, raised money to build a wharf. Because they came from a variety of townships they couldn't agree on which township to name the port after. Eventually they compromised and called it Port Union. But unlike the other ports which lost business to the railways, Port Union's busy days came when the Grand Trunk Railway arrived in 1856 and built its tracks right along the water. Because the tracks rose steeply both to the east and to the west, the railway needed a fleet of helper engines to haul the trains up the grades. The puffing steam engines were kept on sidings at Port Union, where a street plan was laid out. A boarding house as well as a station and several houses were added. Eventually larger engines came into use, and helper engines were no longer needed. Port Union, however, retained its station until the late 1960s. Within the last two decades Scarborough's urban boom has swept up to the fringes of old Port Union, and will soon obliterate it completely. Near the two surviving buildings, the sidings sit rusting and overgrown. Meanwhile, a short distance along the tracks, a modern GO Transit station has replaced the turn of the century GT building.

LAKE HURON

Port Bruce

This community, along with a sister community named Malta, were laid out in the rocky harbour of Baie d'Or on Lake Huron. For a few years it shipped lumber and some farm produce until a fateful night in 1860 when the cabins, warehouses and taverns were devastated in a raging fire. The site was then abandoned and the population of about 100 weary and suddenly homeless residents resettled four miles inland at a location that is known today as Tiverton.

Port Blake

A short-lived shipping place with a dock, warehouse and little else, it began its shipping days in 1853 and by 1900 was home to about 100 people. The area today is a busy cottage and summer resort community and the only thing left of Port Blake is the name of the conservation area.

Port Head

A long-lost port that was located five km north of Kincardine, it lasted scarcely a decade. Founded by Captain Duncan Rowan in 1849 it had regular steamer service until 1860. By then Kincardine was proving to be a better port of call, and Port Head faded. Today there is only a ring bolt in a large boulder that was used to moor the ships, although the shoreline is alive with cottages and summer homes.

Port Findlay

From 1885 until about 1892 this was a regular steamer stop on the St. Mary's River east of Sault Ste. Marie. When the CPR completed its line from Sudbury to the Soo, the steamers stopped calling, and today nothing remains.

LAKE SUPERIOR

Jackfish

Few ghost towns offer the number of ghostly relics that Jackfish does. Begun as a fishing colony in the 1870s, it boomed to new life when in the late 1880s the newly opened CPR chose the harbour to shelter its coal dock. A church, school, store and large hotel clung to the rocky cliff overlooking one of the most beautiful harbours on Lake Superior. The place lasted a long time, thriving until the late 1940s when the CPR began to switch from coal to diesel and closed the dock. By then the sea lamprey, a vicious slithery predator, had destroyed the fishery and Jackfish was abandoned. Although the Trans Canada Highway passes within just a couple of kilometres, Jackfish lies totally abandoned, its many empty structures sagging a little more each year.

Port Coldwell

About 25 km west of the mill town of Marathon lie the sad remains of Port Coldwell. Like Jackfish it began as a fishery in a mountainous harbour of unparalleled beauty. The spot was so spectacular that Group of Seven artist Lawren Harris chose it as the subject for a num-

The CPR station at Jackfish replicated a pattern that the railway company used in many Northern Ontario communities.

The railway coal dock at Michipicoten Harbour.

ber of his modernistic landscape paintings. The CPR had a station here, and a number of railway buildings. The community also contained a store and church. Amid the rubble and foundations of its many buildings, only the cemetery, badly overgrown, survives.

Michipicoten Harbour

It isn't a complete ghost, but it comes close. The historic harbour is the site chosen by early 20th century industrialist Francis Clergue. It was he who identified the enormous mineral potential of the mountains around Wawa and built a port here to ship out the iron ore. He added a coal dock for his steam locomotives, and Michipicoten Harbour was one of the busiest places on Superior's north east shore. When the rails were extended south to the mills in Sault Ste Marie, the ore docks were abandoned. Later, when steam engines were replaced by diesel, the coal docks followed. These days, a few residents find it a quiet place to live and reflect upon the harbour's busy industrial days. It lies a few kilometres west of Wawa.

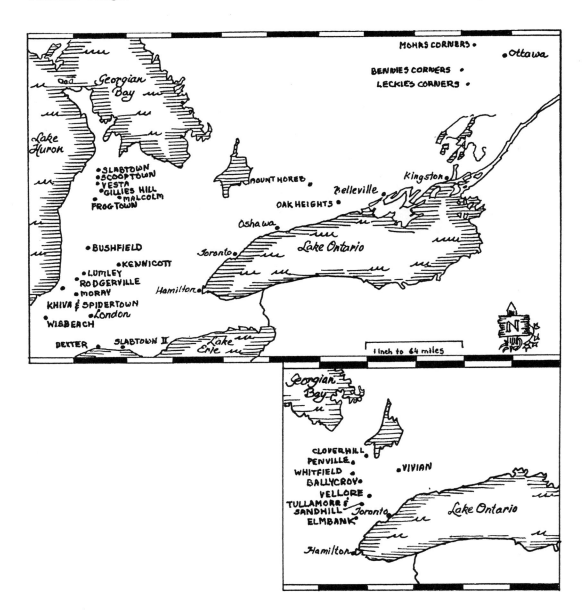

3

Crossroads Hamlets

As the sultry summer air that hung in the little harbour echoed with whack of hammer and axe, a dark and brooding forest stood watch nearby. Pioneer settlers stepped tentatively from the bouncing schooners onto the wooden docks. They arranged their trunks and duffel bags and looked nervously at the towering trees. Somewhere in that mysterious woods lay their dream, their future, their cherished plot of land — the challenge was to get there.

By 1800 Ontario had few roads, and decidedly none that earned praise. Native paths and portages had served as trails for the earliest of the settlers. Some of these became roads that still serve today — Davenport Road and Indian Road in Toronto, and the Hockley Road near Orangeville are among them.

But Upper Canada's first governor, John Graves Simcoe, knew that if he were to settle the territory and provide more protection against Yankee aggression, he needed more roads. In 1799 he sent road-builder Asa Danforth to lay out a route that would link York (now Toronto) with Kingston and Montreal. But Danforth's twisting trail bogged down halfway and was replaced by the more direct Kingston Road.

Few ghost towns lurk here. Both routes eventually evolved into busy roads and the pioneer hamlets that dotted them have ballooned into the urban sprawl that spills endlessly east from Toronto to Cobourg.

Simcoe produced two other roads, the Governor's Road, intended to lead from York to London — it is known as Dundas Street today — and what has become Ontario's best known thoroughfare, Yonge Street. Completed in 1796 between Lake Ontario and Holland Landing, Yonge Street was for most its length little more than a quagmire. One farmer hauling a wagon up the hill into Richmond Hill became so mired that, in disgust, he disassembled his wagon and piled it on the back of his horse.

Simcoe soon extended Yonge Street to Kempenfeld near modern Barrie, and then on up to the British naval garrison on Georgian Bay at Penetanguishene.

To encourage settlers into the wilderness, Simcoe's successors surveyed more trails through the forests: the Gloucester Road angled across the hills of Simcoe County north of Barrie; the Sydenham and Garafraxa Roads penetrated the "Roof of Ontario", as the wind-swept plateaus north of Orangeville are called; Hurontario Street barged straight north from Port Credit to Collingwood. Private settlement roads opened western Ontario, with the Canada Company creating the Huron Road to link Galt with Goderich, and Colonel Tommie Talbot carving the Talbot Road to draw settlers to his land grant south of St. Thomas.

> **Yonge Street**
>
> Much of Canada's most famous street was constructed by the Queen's Rangers in 1796, under the command of Colonel (later Governor) John Graves Simcoe. Initially running only the 60 km to Lake Simcoe, Yonge Street now runs all the way from the shores of Lake Ontario north to the Ontario-Minnesota border. At almost 1,900 km, it is the longest street in the world.

Despite the promise and the heady optimism, the roads were often little more than mud traps, littered with stumps and beset with yawning chasms of seemingly bottomless quagmires. Despite legislation that forced settlers to spend 12 days a year working on the roads, little improved over a half century. Unable to travel more than six miles in a half day, travellers and settlers had to have all their needs close by. Stopping places, with hotels and taverns, lined the settlement roads at frequent intervals. The Penetang Road had more than two dozen taverns.

The Durham Report of 1849 created the system of municipalities in Ontario that persists to this day. The responsibility of these towns, townships and villages was to take care of the roads. Few did, however. Since so much money was used to fund grants for aspiring railway companies, nothing was left for roads. Even privatization failed as the road companies set up their toll booths, and then simply ignored the deteriorating conditions of the roads.

So dreadful were the roads that nearly every key crossroads collected a cluster of stores, shops and taverns, all to serve the needs of the struggling pioneer settler. Crossroads hamlets were a fixture of rural Ontario. The general store offered groceries, dry goods, and a post office, blacksmiths and harness makers were musts. There were tailors, dressmakers and wagonmakers, and no crossroads hamlet would be complete without a tavern.

Many factors combined to doom the crossroads hamlets and stopping places. The inauguration of rural mail delivery in 1908 meant farmers didn't have to trek to the store for their mail. The spread of the temperance movement closed many of the little corner taverns, and the advent of the factory system of manufacturing made the village shop obsolete. But the railways did most of the damage. Communities that were once days apart by stage, were now only hours from each other by train. Goods could be shipped from mass-producing factories in quantities only dreamed of before. Quickly, the proliferation of rail lines drew new businesses to railside, leaving the unlucky villages as backwaters.

The most important building in any crossroads hamlet was the general store. This example survives near London in Southwestern Ontario.

A few clung to life with their churches, schools and remaining residents. Many gained new life with the Car Age and the popularity of country living which followed the Second World War. Others, however, vanished, leaving vacant buildings, foundations or simply vague cellar holes to tell this story of the once pioneer life in Ontario.

Penville

Located near Tottenham, east of County Road 55, Penville began life in 1832 and soon acquired five stores, three taverns and a township hall. What commenced as a peaceful argument would end up in a tavern in a war of fisticuffs in this typically rowdy, rural place. By the 1850s the population stood at 150 and most looked forward to the annual fair. "The show was large", one local commentator wrote, "with about eleven entries of fall wheat, ten of spring, and 12 span of working horses that equalled any shown in Toronto."

Then in the 1870s when the Hamilton and Northwestern Railways passed through Tottenham to the west, Penfield faded from existence. A small cluster of houses is all that remains.

35

Clover Hill

A farm hamlet of 150 in 1895, Clover Hill straddled Highway 89 three kilometres west of Cookstown. The community once boasted an Orange Lodge, and the Dominion Hotel, as well as a general store.

Bennies Corners

An early crossroads village near Lanark, Bennies Corners could once claim a school, general store with a post office and a blacksmith shop. Nearby, where the Indian River enters the Mississippi, stood Stephen Young's barley mill, and a short distance up the Indian River, John Baird's grist mill, the Mill of Kintail. Today only the school and Baird's mill, now the Tait MacKenzie Museum, survive.

Leckie's Corners

An early hamlet near Almonte, the place began in the 1830's when Thomas Leckie opened his general store. The place soon added a dressmaker and a tannery. Only the former tannery remains.

Mohr's Corners

One of the names associated with the Ottawa River was that of John Mohr. It is not too surprising that a few places have the family name. On the river there is Mohr's Landing, and a mile south of the river,

Not much remains in Mohrs Corners compared to when it was the centre of the region.

near the village of Galetta, is Mohr's Corners. It began with a hotel erected by Charles Mohr, and prospered when stage travel was the only form of transport. The hamlet soon added a school, church, two stores and a township hall. But when the railways passed through Galetta and ignored Mohr's Corners, the hamlet faded. Many of the buildings were demolished, while the hall was moved and reconstructed at a nearby farm. Today only a house and the former school survive.

Lumley

Located about six kilometres southeast of Hensall, Lumley was a busy little town in the later years of the 19th century. By 1870 it had a general store, with a dance hall above, a woollen factory, a pump factory, a cooper, a tailor, a shoemaker and a blacksmith. Like many communities its size it also had a debating club whose topics would not be out of place today: "resolved that the press has more influence than the pulpit; resolved that free trade would be more beneficial to Canada than protection".

By 1900 the railways had bypassed Lumley in favour of Hensall and the more efficient factory system had replaced the local craftsmen. Today all the old buildings are gone, save the school which has been transformed into a modern home.

Rodgerville

Rodgerville began as a strategic stopping place on the busy road that connected London with the then remote port of Goderich. Teamsters urging their teams through the quagmire that passed for 19th century roads welcomed the warmth of the lights that flickered through the windows of the Western Hotel, knowing that inside the innkeeper, Matthew Rodgers, had a hot meal and refreshing jug of beer waiting for them. Business directories of the day listed no fewer than two dozen businesses in Rodgerville, among them storekeepers, blacksmiths, and shoemakers and Andrew Malcolm's cheese factory.

The fate that befell Rodgerville was not unusual. In 1876 the surveyors for the London Huron and Bruce Railway appeared. Instead of laying out a station ground at Rodgerville, they chose a location a few miles north and called it Hensall. One by one Rodgerville's bus-

Stagecoaches were the earliest form of transportation and took travellers on bone-jarring trips.

nesses succumbed to the lure of the railway and moved. Today a solitary house and a sign that says simply "Rodgerville, 1845-1890" are all that survive.

Khiva

Among the busier of the settlement roads that lead into the backwoods of Huron County, the Grand bend to Crediton road and the Dashwood to Mount Carmel road, saw much of the traffic. Right where the two crossed stood the hamlet of Khiva. It all began with William Holt's log tavern. A couple of years later a mill owner named Ratz added saw and grist mills. A general store, with the usual post office, and a couple of blacksmiths soon came along, and Khiva was another busy crossroads hamlet. Polling booths for local elections were placed in the hotel where candidates waited with their pile of two-dollar bills to ensure that voters saw it "their" way. A number of workers' cabins were built around the Ratz mills as well. Gradually the businesses declined and shortly after the turn of the century the hotel was demolished and today nothing remains of the pioneer hamlet. Although Huron County Roads 2 and 4 remain busy routes, few who travel bother to give a thought to the silent intersection between them.

Spidertown

Not far from Khiva was the tiny hamlet with the strange name of Spidertown. Even local histories do not record how it got that name. But here at a crossroads just west of Mount Carmel was a store, a doctor's office and a few houses. By the First World War everything of Spidertown had disappeared — even the name.

Bushfield

The land between Brussels and Blyth is lush and rolling. Grain waves in the late summer breeze and cattle graze lazily in green pastures. Here at a quiet country intersection (Lot 10 Con 8) stood the little hamlet of Bushfield. Typical of such places, it had a store, Catholic church and Holland's Hotel. A few shops and houses rounded out the corner. Gradually the place dwindled and one by one the buildings disappeared. Nothing survives but the cemetery.

Wisbeach

The main settlement road from London west to Sarnia was the Egremont Road. About halfway along there was a little hamlet called Wisbeach. The tiny settlement consisted of a store, blacksmith and a few houses, and that was all. Even the population figure of 50, as it was listed in the contemporary directories, was considered generous. Today it is just another vanished crossroads village on Highway 22 just east of Highway 7.

Moray

Drivers hurrying north from Parkhill on Highway 81 little realize that the distance that they cover in 10 or 15 minutes, in pioneer times may have taken half a day. For that reason a little hotel called the "Free Trade Inn" (a crystal ball gazer perhaps?) halfway between Parkhill and Corbett, was welcome indeed. The place grew over the years and added another hotel, store, three blacksmiths and several sawmills, many of which had their own cluster of crude cabins for the mill hands. It had a population listed as 125. The hotels have all burned down, and the stores and shops demolished or moved. Moray now is nothing more than a name on a few old maps, and a memory in the minds of a few oldtimers.

Kennicott

As traffic flows quickly along the wide and quiet Highway 23 north of Stratford, it passes a large, white building. A long-standing land mark, it is the Longeway Hotel, once one of several buildings that had formed the village of Kennicott. Here on the busy pioneer settlement road were two hotels, Gault's store, a blacksmith and sawmill. Temperance legislation closed down the hotels, and time took its toll on the stores. As long as it survives, the hotel will be the sole custodian of the memory of this long vanished hamlet.

Slabtown

While there was never much more to Slabtown than a general store and sawmill, the name reflects the humour and forthrightness that Ontario's pioneer settlers put into their place names. A few wood cabins made of slabs housed the sawmill workers and gave the community its name. Eventually when the trees were gone, the mill was moved away and later demolished, as was the store. Only the grove of trees that surrounded the store remain from the tiny pioneer community. The site is on Highway 21 about six kilometres east of Southampton.

Slabtown II

Located six kilometres south of Aylmer near Lake Erie, this "Slabtown" had more businesses and even more names than its Bruce County counterpart. Maps show it today as being "Luton", a name it acquired when the post office opened. Earlier it had been known as "Newton" after a pioneer family and then Centreville. The former was dropped when the family moved away, the latter when postal authorities realized that there were several other communities by that name.

Its list of businesses was larger as well. Huddled around the crossroads were the typical craftsmen: cabinet maker, shoemaker, wagon maker and blacksmith, plus a hotel and a pair of general stores. Its industries included a sawmill, a cider mill, a cheese factory and on the nearby Silver Creek a grist mill. A place this size usually earned a church and school, and Slabtown was no exception.

With the rise of Aylmer nearby on the busy Air Line Railway

Nearly every creek that flowed in Ontario was an "old mill stream". To serve the needs of the early pioneers for lumber and for wheat, nearly every stream that could supply water-power boasted a mill of some kind.

(later absorbed and then abandoned by the CN) Slabtown dwindled. Today only the church, one of the general stores, and a portion of the hotel linger. Countryside sprawl has crept into the area and a number of newer houses now detract from any ghostly aura Slabtown might have had.

Dexter

They didn't realize it at the time, but the wharves and warehouses that ringed the harbour of Port Stanley would be a metropolis compared to what arriving settlers would discover at Dexter. After they had heaved their trunks from the bobbing schooners and onto the rough horse or ox drawn wagon, they lurched east along the shore road the gut-wrenching six kilometres to a huddle of coarse wooden buildings that would be their home. Among them were the shops of the wagon maker, the blacksmith and the cooper, the general store and the hotel. This in 1850 was Dexter. When the railway reached Port Stanley, Dexter began to fade.

But today anyone driving along County Road 24 between Port Bruce and Port Stanley could drive right past without realizing that this now quiet crossroads was the centre of activity for many pioneer families and farmers. Port Stanley, by contrast, remains a busy harbour while the railway now known as the Port Stanley Terminal Railway, has become a popular tourist attraction.

Frogtown

Located where the Durham Road intersected the Southampton Road, about five kilometres west of Walkerton, it was not surprising that Frogtown developed as a stopping place. Settlers making their way from Guelph into the wilderness then known as the "Queen's Bush" always found rest and refreshment here. As well as the basic hamlet businesses, Frogtown was home to about a dozen families. But as the railways arrived, and as other roads were built and improved, Frogtown lost its strategic advantage and disappeared. Today only a few foundations tell that Frogtown existed at all.

Scooptown

If wood shingles were not available, pioneer home builders would simply scoop out logs, split them and then lay them on the roof frame. The lower layer would be placed scooped side up, while the second layer, scooped side down, would overlap the lower layer. With all five houses in Scooptown constructed in this way, the scattered rural community earned this nickname. Not a hamlet as such, the settlement consisted of families settling on five 20 acre lots carved

What is an easy hill into "Mount" Horeb presented an obstacle to horse-drawn stage coaches.

from a single farm. Such parcels were too small to be economical as farms, and the lots were reamalgamated into a single operation, and the cabins taken down. The place was about 14 km north east of Paisley in western Ontario.

Vesta

Once a popular gathering spot for early farmers, Vesta offered a carriage maker, a wagon maker, a blacksmith, a cooper and a barber. Farmers would wander into the general store to pick up their mail or stagger out of the log tavern after a few drinks too many. All these buildings are gone now, as has the old church. Only the school, two kilometres south, survives to remind today's generation that there was anything here at all. A few maps still show Vesta on County Road 19, seven kilometres west of Chesley.

Mount Horeb

Stagecoach drivers of the 1840s, and 1850s cursing at their teams struggling up the hill into Mount Horeb, would acknowledge that the name "mount" fit. Finally the panting horses halted at the summit in front of one of the two hotels. Here too were a couple of stores, three shops and a number of simple frame homes. Nearby were two churches and a school.

A number of the original structures still survive, although the shops and stores no longer hear the clomp of customers' boots, and modern cars easily slide up what is to today's drivers no slope of any consequence. This collection of pioneer buildings is on Victoria County Road 31, three kilometres east of Highway 35.

Vivian

This forgotten hamlet contains what many might consider to be the most attractive building in any of Ontario's ghost hamlets. It is the beautiful Vivian general store. The hills that surrounded the crossroads were steep and rolling, but that did not entirely discourage pioneer settlers, for those hills were also covered in tall stands of white pine, a resource prized probably even more than level and loamy soil. In fact, when the clearing of the forests was at its most frenzied, 15 sawmills operated in and around Vivian.

Fortunately for heritage enthusiasts the Vivian store has survived.

Travellers on the dirt road in 1883 were relieved when the stage finally jingled to a halt in front of Jonathan Randall's Green Bush Hotel, for after a half day of bouncing over boulders and in and out of mudholes that plagued the road through the pine hills, the rest and refreshment were like a godsend.

But tired though they were, most would have marvelled at what they saw across the road. There stood Robert McCormick's general store, tall and begabled, with ornate fretwork and arched windows. The corners of the yellow brick building were highlighted with designs of red brick.

Vivian's prosperous years were short. The pine was soon ruthlessly stripped away, and the soils that lay beneath proved to be sandy and infertile. After a few years of good harvests, the farmers found that the soft soils were exhausted and had turned into a blowing desert. Many moved away leaving the area largely deserted. Today only the store, no longer open, survives. Thanks to far-sighted conservationists, the blowing sands in 1924 were replanted and are once again cloaked in pine. Newer country homes have moved onto the lands once occupied by the weary farmers, and these owners too marvel at the store. Vivian is located on Highway 48 at Davis Drive.

Vellore

No one knows for sure whether Alexander Muir was humming his composition "The Maple Leaf Forever" when he finished his teaching day at the tiny brick Vellore public school. Not too many years, later, however, many Canadians were humming it, and later pushing for its adoption as a national anthem for Canada.

In Muir's day the community also contained the usual general store with its post office, blacksmith, cooper and wagon maker as well as a township hall and a church, and a number of small wooden houses. The farmland was good, and Vellore prospered. It's death, like its life, was typical of farm hamlets, dying when railways, and later the automobile, made such places obsolete.

As Toronto's Vaughan suburbs lurk on the near horizon, Vellore's old hall and church still survive, and fittingly, host meetings of the local historical society. They stand on the east side of Weston Road a short distance north of Rutherford Road.

> **The Stump Act**
>
> In 1800 Simcoe enacted the Stump Act. Under this law anyone convicted of drunkenness was required to remove a stump from the road.

Whitfield

When Hurontario Street was cut from Port Credit to Collingwood in 1848, its condition was so poor that stopping places were needed at frequent intervals. As pioneers cleared away the woodlands and began cultivating their crops, the roads remained dismal, and pioneers couldn't go very far for their daily needs. Whitfield was one of those places that began as a stopping place and evolved into a small crossroads hamlet. The crossroads eventually acquired a blacksmith an Orange Lodge, and a church.

Eventually travel along the settlement road declined, and in the 1870s when the Hamilton and Northwestern Railway passed nearby it stopped altogether. Years later the province's highway builders chose a route further west for Highway 10 to follow and Whitfield became a forgotten backwater. All that survives at the intersection are the church and the building that housed the Orange lodge. These lie on County Road 17 about six kilometres east of Highway 10.

Gillies Hill

From the settlement roads the settlers trudged into the dark woods.

Small, stump-filled clearings gradually grew into waving wheat fields and farm hamlets seemed to appear at every main intersection. Gillies Hill had the basics and little more: a store with a post office, a township hall, a blacksmith and a church and school. Its peak years were from 1870 to about the time of the First World War. After that cars could carry farmers to larger towns to shop and Gillies Hill faded away, and now today only the vacant school and church survive. Descendants of the pioneers have erected a cairn in memory of those that settled the area and for whom Gillies Hill was their community centre. It is on County Road 10 north of the village of Chesley.

Malcolm

One of many crossroads hamlets that dotted the farmlands of Bruce County, Malcolm could claim during its peak years a hotel, store, church, school, community hall and wagon factory. A few houses also huddled about the intersection. Today the school (now a house), a cemetery and a pair of vacant structures yet linger, although rural sprawl emanating from nearby Hanover, 15 km south, threatens to obliterate Malcolm's ghostly aura.

Tullamore

It began early as a stopping place on what is now the busy Airport Road. But in a time when Toronto was still two day's travel away, Tullamore had a hotel, store, wagon factory, a school, church and several simple homes. Despite its prosperity, one traveller dismissed it as a "miserable tumble down dilapidated place," and that was before it became a ghost town.

With the coming of rail and then cars to drive area farmers to larger towns, Tullamore lost most of its functions. The hotel burned in the 1930s, and the old store was replaced by a gas station. Now a new restaurant and donut shop have restored its role as an area focus, and newer houses have replaced the tiny pioneer cabins.

Signs promising new zoning bylaws appear along the roadside, announcing the approach of look-alike housing and massive malls. Until then Tullamore remains a ghostly image of a once busy crossroads village.

Sandhill

Tullamore's Airport Road neighbour, Sandhill early on in its existence had a tavern, three blacksmiths and three churches. It soon added a general store with the customary post office. Today the intersection is marked with one of the churches and a few of the tiny cabins that the pioneers once called home. One by one, however, these are being replaced with the monster homes that are the trend of the 1990s.

Grahamsville

Up until the 1970s, Grahamsville contained old cellar holes and a pair of vacant homes, all that survived of the tavern, store and other functions of this early crossroads hamlet. In fact, by 1819 Thomas Graham had one of the area's first taverns in full swing and gave the place its name. Donut stores and a gas station have brought new functions to the intersection of Airport Road and Steeles Avenue, while the graveyard alone remains from pioneer times.

Elm Bank

Sharp-eyed flyers taking off from Pearson Airport might observe near the control tower a little cemetery. Close by, tall trees enclose weedy yards. Now part of the airport, these are the ghosts of Elm Bank. It was named by John Grub, a Scottish immigrant, in 1831. The crossroads hamlet quickly added a school, a carpenter, a blacksmith, a church and temperance hall. While most of these functions vanished over time, a few buildings still stood when in the 1960s the airport expanded westward. Now the only thing to disturb the ghosts of the hamlet is the roar of departing jets.

Ballycroy

The busiest intersections were likely to attract a larger than average clutch of businesses, and the corner of the Orangeville and Toronto roads did just that. By the 1830s, Ballycroy's three hotels were doing a thriving business with travellers and with the area's Irish settlers. In a nearby gully hummed a saw and grist mill. A pair of stores and a blacksmith catered to the farmers' other needs. The arrival of the railway to Palgrave in the 1870s, 10 km south, began Ballycroy's

47

The old false fronted general store in Ballycroy is a photographer's delight.

death knell ringing. A few years later one of the hotels burned, killing three female residents; it was never rebuilt. The second hotel was demolished in the 1970s by an adjacent property owner. The third survives with the false-fronted former general store attached.

The once busy pioneer roads have been bypassed by Highways 9 and 50, and the old Orangeville Road is now little more than a gully with foundations lining it.

Would anyone know there was a crossroads hamlet here were it not for this simple sign post?

Oak Heights

The name fits, for this windswept highland between Lake Ontario and Rice Lake was once covered with sturdy oak trees. A pair of churches and a general store gave the area settlers a few of their needs, but over time they vanished completely. To celebrate the historic hamlet, someone has put up a small and simple sign saying "Oak Heights." Without it, no one would ever know that this quiet country crossroads was once a small pioneer centre.

Lemieux

The government removed Lemieux from the face of the earth, and that was probably a good idea. If they hadn't, the earth would have done it for them. Lemieux was a peaceful French Canadian farm community that slumbered on the banks of the South Nation River east of Ottawa. Its problems began, not in Ontario, but 500 miles away in Quebec, in a town called St. Jean Vianney. There in 1971, torrential rains caused the earth to quiver and then collapse, carrying with it 12 homes and 33 hapless victims. The cause lay in a rare subsurface layer of clay called Leda Clay, that when saturated turned into the consistency of soup. Experts from the South Nation Conservation Authority discovered to their horror that the same demon soil lay under Lemieux. Between 1989 and 1990 the authority bought and removed the village's 28 houses and demolished the stone church. It couldn't have come too soon, for just 3 years later the town's main road suddenly slipped away as well. Although the only victim was a badly shaken truck drive who suddenly found himself in a liquid ravine, the slide washed 28 hectares of land into the South Nation River. Today a silent sidewalk leads past Lemieux's empty yards, while in the centre of the onetime town, a cairn commemorates yet another vanished village.

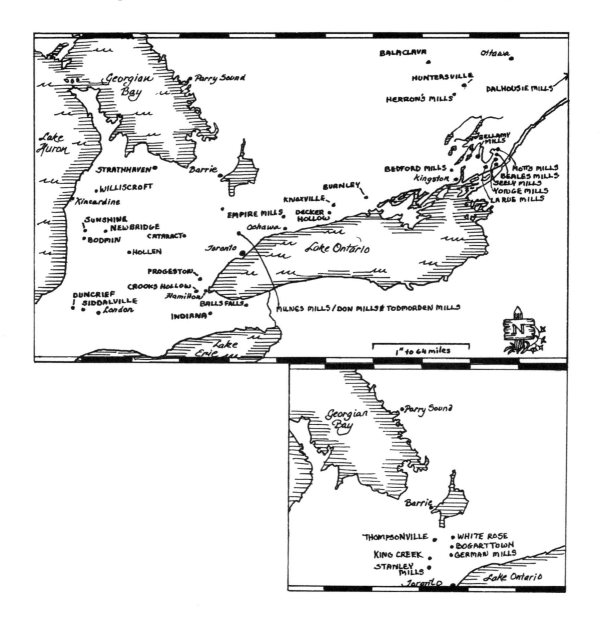

4

By The Old Mill Stream

A mere 200 hundred years have passed since Ontario was covered by a dense forest; still, dark, and to the new arrivals, forbidding and myste-rious. These were the United Empire Loyalists, fleeing the post-revo-lutionary persecutions of the victorious Americans. With no roads other than the native trails and portages, the forest was a formidable barrier to their set-tlement. The only highways were the lakes and the larger rivers and it was along them that the Loyalists settled and Ontario's first mills appeared. A handful of wind-powered mills served the French settlements around Windsor during the 1750s. However, the first industrial mills were sawmills, built and operated by the government to help the Loyalists build their first houses and barns. The first of these settlements was that built in 1782-1784 at the Kingston Mills. These were followed quickly by mills at Napanee, Glenora and at Port Rowan (where the Backus Mill still stands, preserved in a conser-vation area). But throughout Ontario, the forest was still in the way.

Intimidating though it was, the forest offered two conflicting benefits. The canopy of trees acted as a giant cooler, slowing the spring snow-melts and pro-tecting the summertime water tables. This allowed even the tiniest of streams to run year-round, and provide a reliable source of water-power for mill own-ers. But the trees themselves were valuable as timber. The tall pine trunks were especially cherished for masts on British ships as well as for planks in buildings, while oak, maple, and cedar were used for furniture. However, once the trees were gone, so was the protection for the mill streams. In the spring, snow melted rapidly, creating raging torrents that washed away mill dams and even the mills themselves, while in the summer, with the water table now lowered, the mill owners would watch helplessly as the streams slowed to a trickle and often dried altogether.

Gradually the native trails widened into wagon roads, and new roads were hacked through the mosquito-ridden woods. Settlement crept inland, and with it the insatiable need for mills. Few pioneer settlements would survive long without them. Sawmills were usually the first, for the need for lumber was immediate. Later, once the fields had been cleared and grain sowed, the grist mills appeared. Places with more reliable water-power would often see the appearance of flour mills, woollen mills and carding mills, and become Pioneer Ontario's first urban centres.

As the timber vanished, the sawmills were often the first to go as well, and only in those parts of Ontario where forest stands survived, did sawmills continue to operate. Ontario's grist mills lasted much longer. While many converted to steam, a more reliable source of power than water, others used water-power to the end — a very few still do.

Whatever the kind of mill, men, and in carding or woollen mills, women, were needed to work in them. And these workers needed accommodation. For those who couldn't walk from their farms, the owners would provide boarding houses or cabins. These were crude

What is a mill?

If we haven't seen them, we have at least heard about them. Not very many operating mills survive, and those that do are usually found preserved in a conservation area. The purpose of a mill was to clean the grain, and separate the kernel and grind it to flour. When the farmer pulled up with his horsedrawn wagon (although in the very early days pioneers would often walk for miles with the grain sack on their back), the miller would weigh the sack and set aside his share. He would then dump the wheat down a chute to a hopper for storage. From the hopper the grain was taken to the top floor where a revolving screen known as a "smutter" would spin off the dirt and twigs (smut), and then a screen would separate the kernels. From here the kernels were sent down another chute to the grindstones to be crushed into flour.

An early grist mill marks the site of Ontario's first mill at what is today known as Kingston Mills

and drafty, and rent for them was deducted from the workers' pay, often leaving them with little to take home to their families.

Even the smallest of mills became the focus for busy villages, as stores, taverns and other pioneer shops would locate near them. Some grew large enough to attract the attention of the railway builders and many early Ontario mill towns became the cities of today. Most mill villages, however, were ignored by the railways, and while the railside towns boomed, these mill towns became forgotten backwaters. As the mills shut down, the only reason for the village's existence ended. Many became quiet, residential bedroom communities for larger towns nearby. Others vanished, leaving cellar holes and the remains of the old mill dams as the only reminders of how important they had been in the development of Ontario.

La Rue Mills

Tourists driving east from Gananoque on the scenic Thousand Islands Parkway will encounter a blue and orange historic marker announcing "La Rue Mills." Here was one of Ontario's first mills, erected in the 1780s by the government for the United Empire Loyalists. While the little stream still tumbles through the steep, wooded gully, there are no mills in sight, not even the dam. The little pioneer cemetery serves as the solitary reminder of this inconspicuous but important spot.

Bellamy Mills

As roads opened the interior of Eastern Ontario, settlers began to clear the dense woods. By 1798 they had begun a second tier of townships back from the St. Lawrence River and here John Livingston dammed a small creek and built a grist mill. By the middle of the 19th century it could boast a sawmill, a shingle mill, and Chauncey Bellamy's new three-storey grist mill. In addition, there stood a cheese factory, a church and several houses. Then in the 1870s when the Brockville, Westport and Sault Ste. Marie Railway passed several miles to the south through Athens, Bellamy Mills began a steady decline. Located on County Road 9 west of Highway 29, only the gully, the mill pond and the cemetery remain, along with a handful of old houses.

Beales Mills

Because the early settlement roads were so pitiful, settlers en route to their homesteads would take to the lakes and rivers wherever they could. The long, slender channels of Charleston Lake proved to be a perfect alternative to the muddy trails and Charleston grew as a head for navigation. Beales Mills was the best mill site in the vicinity, with a small waterfall tumbling over a rocky precipice. It was good enough to power a saw and grist mill and soon added a store and a few homes. But railways and improved roads ended Lake Charleston's days as a navigation route, and farmers, frustrated from trying to grow crops on the poor soils, switched to raising cattle instead. With the forests gone, the river slowed to a trickle and Beales Mills fell silent. Today only a pair of old dwellings survive and lie south of County Road 40 just a few kilometres east of Charleston, which today lingers on as a small resort community.

Motts Mills

In a low-lying part of Leeds and Grenville County, far from the busy highways, lie the few forgotten homes that once made up the community of Motts Mills. The place was never more than a mill town with a sawmill, a shingle mill and a flour mill. A store and a school are located there as well. But the small flow of Hutton Creek could not withstand the clearing of the forests, and the mills closed. Now only a few houses remain. They are on County Road 7, eight kilometres north of Toledo.

Seeley Mills

The weedy gully beside the crossroads on County Road 32 just north of Lyn is misleading. To the casual observer, nothing could ever have existed here. Yet not only was the place a small but active mill town, it was a station stop on the Brockville, Westport and Sault Ste. Marie branch of the Grand Trunk Railway. At that time it could boast a school, hotel, the mills and the small, wooden station. But even the railway could not save the place from the diminishing flow of water in the creek, and Seeley became just a whistlestop on the line. Only the hotel outlasted the closing of the line in the 1940s and remained as a ruin into the late 1970s.

Yonge Mills

It didn't take the Loyalists long to discover a water-power site on Jones Creek about a mile inland from the St. Lawrence. Not only that, but the creek was navigable for small boats to the river itself, then the region's most important "highway". In the 1850s, the Grand Trunk Railway built their main line nearby and Yonge Mills became a busy farm town and station stop. By the 1870s it could claim a sawmill, a fulling mill (similar to a carding mill), a store, and a pair of blacksmiths, as well as a couple of hotels. Today the original mill site is a quiet, wooded gully beside Highway 2, while the station village, with only a church, vacant section house, and the station (now a garage on a nearby farm), lies on County Road 23 about a kilometre north of Highway 2.

Bedford Mills

Perhaps it was its location on two busy transportation routes that made this mill town one of Eastern Ontario's most prosperous among what would become ghost towns. While the Perth Road provided a settlement route from Kingston northward to Perth, the Rideau Canal opened a water route from Kingston to Ottawa. Although the area today resembles a wooded and rocky wilderness, in 1831 it was a community of farms. Here, where Buttermilk Falls tumbles from Devil Lake into the Rideau Canal, John, George, and William Chaffey (after whom Chaffey Falls was named) built saw and grist

Bedford Mills on the Rideau Canal is popular with photographers.

55

mills, a boarding house, cabins and a store. Eventually the place even had its own power plant. Later the Tetts opened up a few mica mines and Bedford Mills became one of the busiest centres around.

But soon the trees were gone and the railways bypassed the place, a fate much the same as befell other mill towns like it. The mines ran out of deposits, the soils proved useless for modern farming, and Bedford Mills became a ghost town. With historic marker on County Road 10 pointing the way, Bedford Mills has a few things to see — the white frame church, the stone mill (now a house), and the ruins of the flume and power plant. Grass and trees now occupy the site of the sawmill, the store and the old cabins.

Herron's Mills

The mills here, five kilometres north of Lanark, were started by John Gillies who in 1842 built a sawmill, grist mill, oatmeal mill and carding mill on the Clyde River. Soon after, the place added a store, blacksmith and school. In 1871 John Gillies sold the operation to John Herron, after whom the place at last took its name. The Gillies' had other things in mind and soon became one of the premier lumbering families in Ontario. Meanwhile the mills at his old home town eventually shut and Herron's Mills became a ghost town. The his-

Historic Herron's Mills now lies abandoned.

56

toric Gillies house remains occupied, but the mills, store and school closed down, leaving only an abandoned house and mill building.

Balaclava

Balaclava remains one of Ontario's more photogenic relic mill villages. It all started in 1855 when Duncan Ferguson and Donald Cameron built grist and saw mills on the rushing waters of Constan Creek about 30 km west of Renfrew. Nearby stood the brooding Black Donald Mountains and the Opeongo Colonization Road that led to them. With its store, hotel and blacksmith shop, Balaclava remained a busy industrial centre for the surrounding farmers. But when the railway builders chose a route through Hyndford several miles to the north, and when the farmlands in the unrelenting mountains failed, Balaclava's business declined. Nevertheless, it clung stubbornly to life and the sawmill continued to operate on water-power until 1967. Although

The remains of Balaclava should be preserved, but nothing has been done so far.

the hotel burned in the early 1990s, the store, blacksmith and mill still stand as ghostly ruins, and intriguing subjects for the amateur photographer.

Dalhousie Mills

Another photogenic ghost town, Dalhousie Mills, north of the historic St. Lawrence River town of Lancaster, began when Charles Stackhouse built his mills on Rivière Delisle Creek in Eastern Ontario, almost within a "bonjour" of the Quebec border. A street pattern was laid out with lots lining a side street that led west from the main road and down to the mill. A hotel, store, blacksmith and other buildings lined the main street (now County Road 23), and a second side street that led east. While the mill is long gone, replaced by the "round" church, and the old lots on the mill street now support new homes, the store sits empty, and the other side street contains ghostly vestiges of this onetime mill town.

Huntersville

Another long-gone and long-lost mill village, Huntersville was situated on a branch of the Indian River near Clayton, west of Ottawa. Here James and Alex Hunter built a woollen mill which at its peak employed 20 men, a large operation for its time.

Decker Hollow

Decker Hollow is one of those places that makes the pursuit of vanished villages so much fun. It's exact whereabouts and history are a bit of a mystery. Research by Harold Reeve published in the "History of the Township of Hope" suggests that the place was founded by the Decker family and prior to 1870 had a sawmill, a grist mill, store, Dan Decker's tavern, a blacksmith shop and several houses. Its demise must have been speedy for the county atlas published in the 1890s shows only a solitary, unidentified building on the site, and no trace of the Decker name. A map published in the 1920s likewise shows just one structure which it labels "sawmill (old)". Today Decker Hollow, or Deckerville, as it was also known, is hard even to get to. The once busy mill road is now just a trail through a pasture while the site of the mill and mill pond is a tangle of swampy underbrush. Its location is about four kilometres southwest of Elizabethville which is on Durham Regional Road 9.

Knoxville

There's not much left of Knoxville, for most of the buildings had vanished by the early 1900s. However, in its prime it contained nearly a dozen houses, a church and the mill, which lasted only from 1881 until 1895. The location is marked as Lots 6 and 7, Concession 6, Hope Township.

Empire Mills

Ever since settlement proceeded inland from Port Oshawa, the flat and fertile farmlands supported a vibrant agricultural economy. Mills were nestled in the little gullies, for there were no large rivers here, and on the plains between, wheat waved golden in the breeze, and dairy cattle munched lazily in the green pastures. Farm hamlets with names like Brooklin and Columbus were centres for farmers.

Between these two, there hummed a busy little mill town. Its name was Empire Mills, owned by the Matheson and Ratcliffe firm, and claimed by some to be the largest in the area. "An East Whitby Mosaic" by Elsie Cleverdon, tells of 50 men working the mill by 1850. Most were from Yorkshire and Lancashire in England, and lived in small cabins that lined wooden sidewalks. The place also had a store, church, school, and by 1883, electric power — a luxury not yet universal.

The location and remains of Empire Mills still provokes debate among history buffs. County atlases of the day show mills on the east side of what is today Regional Road 52, while a string of houses lined the west side. More mills appeared east of the intersection.

But the railways seemed to go everywhere but Empire Mills. The closest was the Whitby and Port Perry three kilometres to the west, while the Grand Trunk passed through Oshawa itself well to the south. Needing the rails to compete, the firm moved to Markham, and the little mill was reduced to operating with only a handful of men. Finally when the devastating spring floods of 1890 washed through the gully, the place was abandoned.

The only evidence that there was anything other than farms and fields is the cemetery. As new strip development engulfs the area, it will become even harder for amateur archaeologists to track down this elusive ghost.

Burnley

Today Mill Creek rushes unimpeded through a woodland of young cedar trees. But in the mid-1800s when the creek earned its name, there were dozens of mills along it. In 1860 R.H. Grimshaw built saw and grist mills and R. Pringle laid out a townsite which he called Burnley. During its prime it contained the usual blacksmith, store and hotel along with a church, school and community hall. The only other industry was a cheese factory.

By the 1930s grain and cheese production stopped in that area and

Burnley began to decline. By the end of the war only the church, store and community hall still stood. In the '60s the church was torn down, in the 80s the pretty little store. Today, of Burnley's original buildings, only the hall, the cheese factory, which is now a home, and a couple of other houses survive. They lie on County Road 25, seven kilometres east of Highway 45.

Stanley Mills

Today a line of modern monster homes hovers menacingly on the crest of the hill as if they were a row of enemy soldiers ready to charge into the gully and wipe away the last vestiges of Stanley Mills. And soon they will. But until they do the few buildings that survive from this old industrial village can reflect upon its bygone days.

In the 1820s when the forests still covered much of the land, the little creeks which flowed through the gullies carried enough water to attract Thomas Burwell, industrialist and mill builder. Here he locat-

The first Ball residence at Balls Falls, then Glen Elgin, was a simple log cabin.

60

ed his little industrial empire. It included a grist mill, distillery, sawmill, tannery, blacksmith, store, hotel and warehouse. By the 1860s the population stood at more than 200, all because of Burwell. But by the end of the century those flowing streams had slowed to a trickle. Industry was flocking to the new railway lines, and Stanley Mills became obsolete. Only three old buildings remain, and some long lanes that were once the village streets.

Today re-zoning signs appear all along Airport Road in and around Stanley Mills, a firm foreboding that Brampton's urban sprawl is about to sweep away the last vestiges of this old ghost town.

Balls Falls

It's the ghost town with the rhyming name; it's one of the Niagara area's oldest settlements, and it's preserved. It was common in early Ontario for the British government to reward its brave army officers with land. John and George Ball were fortunate in that the 1200 acres they received in 1812 had not just one, but two falls of water, enough power for three mills. They wasted little time in establishing a grist mill at the lower falls, a saw mill at the upper falls and, on the cliff above that, a woollen mill. They laid out a townsite and called their little empire Glen Elgin. Another industry to take advantage of the site was a lime kiln that used the exposed limestone in the cliff.

In addition, it had the usual array of shops, while cabins lined the riverbank between the two falls. A boarding house stood near the woollen mill for the women who made the kerseys, casimires and flannels for which the place became famous.

But when the rails of the Great Western Railway were laid below the escarpment rather than above it, Glen Elgin faded. But not altogether. The old, wooden grist mill and the Ball home managed to survive, preserved now by the conservation authority, and stand beside a pioneer church and cabin brought in from other spots nearby. The little church often hosts weddings. Picnickers lay out their blankets by the river while in the fields above

Casimere & Kersey

The term *casimere* is very likely derived from *cashmere*, which refers to a wool obtained from Kashmir goats in India. But *casimere* (sometimes called *kerseymere*) is a coarse, woollen cloth developed in England and popular in Upper Canada in the 19th century. *Kersey* is a coarse, ribbed and closely napped woollen cloth, deriving its name from where it was originally made: Kersey, in Suffolk, England. For a time, Great Britain led the world in the production and export of wool and wool products.

it, wargamers act out battles of the 1812 conflict, a tribute to the bravery of the two 1812 veterans who created the place.

Hollen

Unlike Balls Falls, this ghost town was nearly destroyed by a conservation authority. When the Grand River Conservation Authority dammed the waters of the Conestoga River 35 km northwest of Kitchener as a flood control measure, they submerged part of the ghost town of Hollen.

The flow of the river early attracted Hugh Hollingshead who built shingle and grist mills, while the fertility of the surrounding farmlands meant that it developed more than the usual number of businesses. More than two dozen enterprises and 400 residents shared the 150 town lots that had been laid out for them. But when the railways came, they ignored Hollen, and gradually the businesses moved away. In 1948 local history writer Hazel Mack, aptly labelled it as a ghost town. Ten years later, with the flood dam in place, the waters began to creep across the townsite, covering the mill foundations and the dam.

While a couple of older houses still stand, newer residences have been built along the shores of the artificial Conestoga Lake and have restored some vitality to the location.

Mills Preserved in Conservation Areas

In 1946, when A.H. Richardson began Ontario's conservation movement, he could not have realized that it would save many of Ontario's heritage sites. Modelled after the Tennessee Valley Conservation Authority, Ontario's conservation authorities are an association of municipalities that share common watersheds. While their main purpose was to prevent floods and conserve soils, they found within their floodlands many historic mills. Many have grown into important tourist attractions on their own. The Bell Rock Mill, north of Kingston, still rumbles away using water-power to cut lumber for area farmers; the Backus Mill, near Port Rowan, is Ontario's oldest surviving mill, still powered by water.

Indiana

On Highway 54 just 15 km south of Caledonia sits Indiana. It has just two signs: one on a garage proclaims "Indiana"; the other, beside it, says "No Trespassing." Beyond the latter prohibition lie the streets and ruins of what was once a busy mill town beside the locks of the long vanished Grand River Canal.

In addition to the historic Welland, Trent and Rideau canals that remain busy today, Ontario has witnessed the building (and abandoning) of many smaller canals — the Newmarket Canal, the Fort Francis Canal, the Root River Canal, and the Grand River Canal. Of

Ontario's vanished canals, the Grand River was the longest.

In the 1830s, when the locks of the Grand River canal swung open for the first time, they attracted small settlements and industries beside them. Located by Lock Station 5, Indiana grew and by 1848 was described by travel writer W.H. Smith as "a small village pleasantly situated on the Grand, with a grist mill, two sawmills, distillery, two stores, two taverns" as well as the usual shops. A town plan was laid out with seven mill sites and 117 lots on 10 streets. By 1870 the place had grown still more to a population of 300 with an impressive list of 30 businesses as schooners glided through the locks.

As usual it was the railways that doomed it. Less and less traffic followed the river and by 1878 another traveller described Indiana as an "old village which grew into importance while the [canal] existed and then dropped into decay and dilapidation".

Now those streets are private driveways and lead to a pair of houses and empty, weedy lots. By the steep riverbank old concrete steps, cracked and festooned with weeds, lead down to the now forested site of Lock Station 5.

Duncrief

By the 1830s settlers had made their way into the heartland of Southwestern Ontario and began to seek out mill sites. On Duncrief Creek, halfway between London and Sarnia, Jeremiah Robson built a sawmill on land owned by the Charlton family. A grist mill soon followed. Never large, Duncrief contained the mills, a blacksmith, a woodworking shop and a store with a post office in it. When the mill burned in 1885, and the then owner J.B. Pethram went broke, the community quickly rallied to rebuild it. The new structure stood four storeys high. But in 1908 when floods washed it away, business was so minimal that it remained stilled forever. Only a house and a vacant building overlook the weedy gully today which lies 15 km northwest of London, north of County Road 16.

Siddalville

On Nairn Creek, not far from Duncrief, stood another mill town, Siddalville. Founded by early land owner John Siddal, the place grew to contain a store, blacksmith, wagonmaker, two hotels, and, conveniently, a brewery. No fewer than six mills sat along the banks of the creek. But the railways killed all that, and today not a stick remains.

Strathaven

It looks like a driveway leading from the red brick Baptist church to a couple of old houses. One of those houses was the Strathaven general store and the laneway leading to it was Strathaven's main street. After J. Thomas and Sons opened their flour, saw and shingle mills on the shore of the Bighead River in Grey County in the 1860s, the road to the site attracted a blacksmith, a wagonmaker and two general stores as well as a church, school and Foresters Hall. But with no railway, Strathaven was doomed to remain a backwater, and, as with most backwaters, it gradually faded. By the time the Second World War broke out the place had lost its industries and one of its stores. Today the school and the other store (the McCessock store) are private homes, while only the church with its manse survive. The old main street now leads from the 8th Concession of Grey County's Holland Township, past the foundations and overgrown yards of yet another of Ontario's ghost mill towns.

Sunshine

Except for the cemetery, Sunshine is one of those places that has vanished with virtually no trace. Founded in 1868 and known first as Providence, Sunshine by the 1890s could claim saw and grist mills, Crittenden's store, Webb's blacksmith shop, and Rogerson's chair factory, and across the road a church with a small cemetery, with a boardwalk linking them all. But when the railway arrived, they missed Sunshine and one by one Sunshine's businesses moved off to railside. Rogerson moved his furniture factory to Blyth in 1887. Vanstone moved the machinery from his mill to Southampton the next year, and the owner of the store closed it and moved to Brussels, all on the new Wellington Bruce and Huron Railway. By 1899 only three houses remained. The church survived but it too closed in 1927. Of this once busy little mill village, south of Huron County Road 16, only grassy fields remain. The little Sunshine cemetery is the only evidence that there was anything here at all.

Bodmin

From Sunshine a side road leads to the next village, Bodmin. Founded in 1855 by William Harris who built on the Maitland River a saw and grist mill, the place soon acquired a store, shoemaker, cabinet factory and a number of houses. Close by, the Bodmin Lime Works advertised "one of the best white limes" in Canada using clay, limestone and wood from the area. But as with its sister village, Sunshine, Bodmin died when the railways passed it by. By 1890 nothing remained. Today it is even hard to find the side road to Sunshine, or even Charlotte Street, the onetime main street on the site.

Newbridge

Like Sunshine, Newbridge was another Maitland River mill town. By the 1880s it had saw and grist mills, stores and a pair of hotels which saw the frequent comings and goings of stagecoaches. A population of 200 lived on a small town plot of 30 lots. Now only the church and a couple of houses remain.

Progreston

For a time it appeared as if this optimistic name was deserved. In the 1870s, this water-power site on Bronte Creek, about 15 km northwest of present day Burlington, had no fewer than three sawmills, two grist mills, a peg factory and blacksmith. A woollen mill and casket factory followed and the place was home to 180 residents. The last of the mills managed to survive until the 1960s.

King Creek

Not far from the little board and batten railway station in King City there stood a thriving mill village on the banks of King Creek. In 1827 Christopher Stokes, a millwright who had migrated from England two decades earlier, built a grist mill on the creek and for a while the place was known as "Stokes Hollow". The industry attracted a flour mill, store and hotel, and an Irish shoemaker named Robert Simpson. The business directories of the day indicated that the population stood at about 100, and that it cost 20 cents to take the stage to the Northern Railway station in King City. Eventually the stores and hotel closed, and the mills fell silent. Most of the remains of these industries were swept away in October of 1954 when the rains of Hurricane Hazel turned the peaceful creek into a foaming torrent. Today picnickers, enjoying what is now the Humber Trails Conservation Area, would never know that it was once a busy mill village. Ironically, the little King station, claimed to be Canada's oldest, survives in the nearby King Museum.

Cataract

Located on the brow of the spectacular Credit River Canyon, Cataract is a ghost town that has come back to life. The site attracted a group of investors to mine a possible salt deposit. Beside the roaring fall, which can be heard a half kilometre away, they built a sawmill and a shantytown of crude shacks and called the place Gleniffer. But the salt

deposit was uneconomical and Gleniffer was abandoned. A few decades later it caught the attention of Richard Church who built a grist mill and laid out a townsite, naming it, modestly, Church's Falls. A few years later, the Credit Valley Railway surveyors realized that the canyon was the only route their railway could follow to surmount the mighty Niagara Escarpment, which here is at its most spectacular. By 1875 the valley was filled with the steam and smoke of the belching steam locomotives. The location became a junction for a branch line that forked off towards Fergus and the town soon bustled with stores, boarding houses, a railway station and sidings and a pair of popular hotels: the Junction House and the Horseshoe Inn.

Shortly before the close of the century John Deagle bought up the grist mill and converted it to a hydro electric generating plant, and by 1905 it was supplying power to locations as far away as Orangeville. The pond above the plant flooded the entire val-

Thundering falls like that at Cataract often attracted industries. The old mill here is now just a ruin.

66

ley. The Deagles sold the operation to Ontario Hydro in 1944 which closed it a mere three years later, moving the equipment to Kagawong on Manitoulin Island. The CPR, which had acquired the Credit Valley Railway many years earlier, objected to proposals to use the pond as a recreational area and it was drained. Later, with the replacement of steam power with diesel, the CPR removed its station and water tank. The boarding houses and stores fell vacant and the place became a desolate ghost town.

But it didn't remain that way for long. Toronto commuters were out looking for country homes, and the view over the canyon attracted their attention. Soon the empty houses and stores had been replaced with newer country homes, and the lone hotel became a popular restaurant. The old road which led down the canyon is now a hiking trail that starts near the hotel. Along it are the now abandoned road bed of the branch line to Fergus, which is also a hiking trail, the stone ruins of the Deagles Power Plant and the thundering cataract that started it all in the first place.

German Mills

Metro's Don Valley, long before the noise and air pollution brought on by the expressway boom, was a peaceful valley of mills. The steady flow of water, the wide valley floor and the nearness of Toronto with its railway access to all parts of Canada, attracted them. Wherever a mill could fit, there was one. Strangely, one of the earliest was nowhere near Toronto, or as it was called then, York. Instead German Mills appeared on a branch of the Don near today's Thornhill.

In 1794 William Berczy, swept up in the heady settlement boom then engulfing the Lake Ontario shoreline, induced a colony of as many as 220 Germans to settle on what was then a distant branch of the Don River. Here they established a sawmill, a grist mill and, naturally, a brewery, and built an unknown number of log cabins. By 1796 the colony found itself short of grain and was surviving chiefly on potatoes and turnips. Despite Berczy's earnest protestations, the government offered no help and in 1805 Berczy was forced to sell the land. By 1828 German Mills was abandoned, and, as an observer of the day remarked, the old mills were reduced to "an impressive sight in the midst of the woods in a deserted condition with their windows all boarded up."

Although the settlement has long vanished, and the river bed altered, the name has survived locally to this day. A street of modern backsplits, German Mills Road runs west from Don Mills Road, south of John Street in Toronto, and ends at an attractive board and batten school surrounded by a picket fence. Although built in the 1840s, long after Berczy's Germans had fled elsewhere, it has survived from an era that has otherwise vanished utterly from the Metro area.

Milnes Mills

The thousands of drivers who rush, or crawl as the case may be, along Toronto's Don Valley Parkway every hour, are unaware that as they steer under the Lawrence Avenue Bridge, they are passing the last house in a ghost town called Milnes Mills (or Milnesville, or Milnes Hollow). In 1832, when this part of the Don Valley was several hours by horse from the muddy little settlement then called York, Alexander Milne chose the site for a saw and woollen mill. Here, where Lawrence Avenue twisted down the steep slope of the valley wall were the mills, the large Milne house, and the 16 cabins of Milnes Mills. By the 1860s the woollen mills were turning out 2,225 yards of cloth per year, and the sawmill more than 400,000 feet of lumber.

Following devastating floods in 1878, the old mill was replaced with a three-storey brick structure and a tenement was built for the workers. But gradually the place disappeared, bit by bit. In 1921 the Milne house burned to the ground and was never rebuilt. In 1946 the mill was dismantled and the bricks used elsewhere. In 1953 the houses were demolished to make way for the planned parkway; and in 1964 Lawrence Avenue was widened into a four-lane artery that crosses the Don Valley Parkway. But on the east side of the valley, the old alignment of Lawrence still twists down the valley wall and ends at the silent, white house, the last vestige of the ghost town of Milnes Mills.

Don Mills

It is now the name of the busiest road intersection in all Ontario. But what were the Don Mills? A map from 1880 shows no fewer than 20 sawmills, five grist mills and a distillery between the forks of the Don

The solid brick mill at Milnes Mills has been replaced by the Don Valley Parkway.

River, between the Don Mills Road and Don Valley Parkway inter-change and Steeles Avenue (the northern limit of today's Metro Toronto). These do not include the busy little mill village at Milnes Mills.

In a hollow, where North York General Hospital sits today, were the saw and grist mills that made up the community of Oriole. Erected by William Gray, the four-storey wooden grist mill was operated by a water-powered turbine, while the sawmill turned out a quarter million feet of lumber every year. Four sawmills were clustered along the Don near Leslie Street and Eglinton Avenue in what is Wilket Creek Park, with three more at Bayview and Lawrence Avenue. Another busy milling area was the site of the Humphrey Mills in the valley east of Don Mills Road, south of York Mills Road. But the busiest of the mill operations were those of the Taylor brothers, with a grist mill, distillery and three paper mills at three locations near the forks of the Don. The largest of these, the Taylor mill, employed more than 100 workers.

With the creation of several Metro parks, the establishment of York University's Glendon campus, and the incursion of the Don Valley Parkway, all traces of these early mills have been utterly obliterated. Only the name remains.

Todmorden Mills

Of all the old mills that once hummed in the valley of the Don River, those known as the Todmorden mills are the only ones that were saved. In 1826 two families from Todmorden, England arrived in York by way of Niagara Falls. They were the Eastwoods and the Helliwells. In that period the governor of Upper Canada had offered a reward for the first entrepreneur to build a paper mill. Following a furious race the Helliwells lost out by mere days to James Crooks of Ancaster. Nonetheless, the site became a major industrial enclave which included the York Paper Mills, a distillery and brewery and several homes. By 1856 the settlement could also claim a shoemaker, carpenter, boarding house, a butcher and the Todmorden House Tavern.

Of all the mills that once filled the Don Valley, only Todmorden Mills has been preserved.

Part of the settlement nestled on the east slope of the valley, the rest strung along the road which hugged the crest of the valley. In those days it was called Don Mills Road; today it is Broadview. A tortuous trail snaked down the hill from the upper settlement to the mills. Today that road is the busy but still twisting Pottery Road. And at the bottom, rising above the trees in the Todmorden Historic Park is the brick chimney of the old brewery, now preserved and used as a community facility. The old Helliwell home has become a museum and archives for those researching the history of the Don Valley.

Crooks Hollow

Surrounded by the urban sprawl that is engulfing the Hamilton and Ancaster area, the little gorge through which the waters of Spencer Creek tumble is like an oasis. As the road twists through the steep, forested gulch it passes (almost imperceptibly) the onetime industrial empire of James Crooks. James Crooks had fled the American invasion of Niagara-on-the-Lake in 1813 to the water-power site on the little creek and built a grist mill, distillery and Upper Canada's first paper mill. By 1830 the little valley hummed with more mills, a farm implement factory and several dwellings. But the arrival of the railway era doomed the village and the industries shut down. The grist mill lasted until it burned in 1934. Happily, it is a ghost town that can be easily explored, for many of the old industry sites and foundations lie within lands owned by the Hamilton Region Conservation Authority.

> **Finding Crooks Hollow**
>
> Within the boundary of Crooks Hollow Conservation Area and along Crooks Hollow Road west of Old Brock Road just north of Dundas Ontario.

Thompsonville

Thompsonville remains to this day a pleasant rural community nestled along the banks of the Nottawasaga River. It was a much different story 150 years ago when Tommie Thompson arrived from Ireland. Here, in what was then only a partly cleared wilderness, Thompson, along with his sons, dammed up the river and built a sawmill, a grist mill and a flour mill. He surveyed the rest of his land into 26 building lots, and Thompsonville was born. The place soon added a store, hotel, and blacksmith as well as a church and Orange Lodge. In 1868 when William Train added mills and houses for his workers, Thompsonville suddenly had a suburb with the name Trainsville. The builders of the Northern Railway in 1877 must have liked the name for it was here, not Thompsonville, that they built a siding for the mill and a wooden platform for the passengers. A few years later when Trainsville disappeared, the little shed known as the Thompsonville Station was built. The village at its peak is estimated to have had 30 places of business.

Today they are gone: the stores, hotel, mills, the station and even the tracks. Only the church and Orange Lodge outlasted them, and now they are gone as well. The community today is a quiet residential suburb southeast of Alliston.

Williscroft

Amid the flat and fertile farmlands of Bruce County, George Williscroft opened a post office in his house. The waters of the Snake Creek were plentiful enough to attract a sawmill and grist mill. Near it were a cheese factory, store and blacksmith, as well as a church, school and Orange Lodge. The usual factors combined to doom the little place — rural mail delivery, the advent of the railways and the car, the predominance of larger urban centres — and today only the school, church and vacant blacksmith shop survive.

The mill wheel — always an impressive sight. Water either passes over the top of the wheel (the overshot wheel), drops onto it (the breast wheel), or flows under it (the undershot wheel). The moving wheel was attached to gears which slowly turned the mill stones (weighing as much as 2000 pounds). As mill technology improved, along came the turbine mill where the water would drop straight down a chute and power a turbine connected to the mill stones. Steam power replaced water power where railway towns were too far from rivers or water sources became less reliable. Fuel was burned to create steam to drive the gears. Steam power was also popular for sawmills but it accounted for many mills burning down. Now, huge mills are powered by electricity and controlled by computer. Yet here and there in rural areas, a few old mills rumble on, using the power of the old mill stream.

White Rose

As cooks pry open their bags of White Rose flour, how many would realize that the name on the flower bag was also given to a community that is today a ghost mill-site. It was located on Leslie Street at the Vandorf Sideroad near Aurora, beside another one of those early mill streams that lasted as long as the forest cover. Jared Lloyd chose this location to built saw and grist mills. Nearby were a store, wagonmaker and temperance hall. In 1886, the forest cover gone, a rampaging spring flood washed away the dam, and the mill operated for a few more years using steam power. The mill was demolished in 1903, and the store was closed in 1913 when rural mail delivery replaced one of its most important community functions. Today, none of the original buildings survive, and not a trace remains of the early mill village with the famous name.

Bogarttown

By contrast, several of Bogarttown's old buildings remain. The place began when an American millwright of Dutch extraction, Martin Bogart, ventured into the woods north of York looking for mill sites. At a spot just south of present-day Newmarket he found what he was looking for and built a sawmill, and later a grist mill. Gradually a busy community began to take shape around the mills, with a store, blacksmith, tailor, carpenter, shoemaker and general store. By the 1850s Bogarttown was in a keen competition with its northern neighbour, Newmarket, when the builders of the Ontario Simcoe and Huron

Railway chose the latter for its station, and Bogarttown quickly faded. But it didn't die altogether, and today a few of its original houses, and the blacksmith, still stand near the corner of Mulock Drive and Leslie Street; an oasis of history in a desert of suburban sprawl.

The fate suffered by this mill was shared by many others when the clearing of the forests caused the rivers to go dry.

Georgian Bay
MOODSTOWN
Ottawa
FRANKTOWN
Lake Huron
OLIPHANT
PORT POWELL
LOCKERBY
WAVERLY
Barrie
LOVAT
Belleville
Kingston
SELDOM SEEN
PRESQU'ILE
Oshawa
Toronto
Lake Ontario
ST. JOSEPH
Hamilton
London
SAXTONTOWN
JAMESTOWN
SUCKERTOWN
Lake Erie
BALDOON
N
1 Inch to 64 miles

5

The Dreamers

As is the case with land speculators today, early Ontario land owners regarded the land not as a precious resource, but as a commodity; something to make them money, big money. Whenever prosperity approached, or seemed to, land increased in value. As settlement crept through the forests, land values around the water-power sites on rivers and streams shot up; as track layers hammered down the rails for the railway lines, values along the rights of way skyrocketed as well. Landowners would often donate land to the railway for station grounds just so their property beside it would rise in value. On this property the owners would lay out their town plans. Most were completely unimaginative — a grid pattern of streets sliced into square building lots, and occasionally a central square.

But most of their ambitious schemes remained simply paper towns. Perhaps it was because the railway builders often changed direction, or because the economy suddenly changed and a town was no longer needed at that location. Changing transportation and unexpected shifts in the political winds both contributed to Ontario's pile of paper towns, and the failed dreams of their promoters.

Presqu'ile
Smothered now by a cottage community within Presqu'ile Provincial Park, Presqu'ile was once destined for greatness. In 1802 the government of the day chose the site, one of eastern Lake Ontario's best harbours, for the capital of Newcastle District (Upper Canada was divided into administrative districts). It put engineers to work designing a town plot and built a courthouse and jail. The jail's first customer, a native, was en route aboard the schooner the Speedy, when a fierce storm blackened the sky and raced down upon the hapless vessel. Everyone aboard was tossed into the foaming waters and drowned.

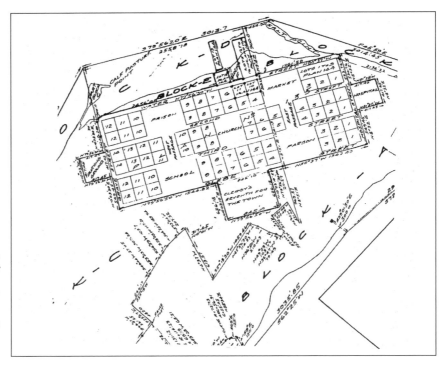

As this plan shows, Presqu'ile was once destined for greatness, as the capital of Ontario's early Newcastle District.

The waves smashed the schooner to pieces and no trace was ever found. On the point the wooden lighthouse, now automated, has guided ships since 1840 and is the second oldest operating lighthouse (the oldest was built in 1808 on Gilbraltar Point in Toronto) on the Canadian side of the Great Lakes. Among the cottages, whose ages vary, lie only two original houses. Disheartened, the government changed its mind and placed the capital in Cobourg instead.

Lovat

Lovat, in Bruce County, was not a total bust. A water-power site of the rushing water of Willow Creek, it attracted sawmills and brickyards, and in 1864 the first post office opened. In 1877 it was clear that the soil was productive and heady optimism permeated the countryside. A large town plan was laid out to accommodate the bustling town that Lovat was sure to become. Several streets with names like Thomas, Albert, Hagett, Lemon and Paisley crisscrossed a two-acre town plot.

Some businesses moved in. Besides sawmills and brickyards there were a store with the usual post office, a hotel and a couple of blacksmiths. However, the usual fate befell these operations. The creek began to run dry and after a few years of steam operation, the mill closed. By 1926 the brickyards shut down, rural mail delivery closed the post office in the general store, and the advent of the Auto Age ended the blacksmiths. Lovat's promising town plan never developed and the place today is a quiet collection of homes in the Ontario countryside.

Port Powell

The early years of the 19th century were heady ones for the southern shores of Georgian Bay. Great log booms were being hauled in from the pine forests far across the bay. Large sawmills hummed in nearly every cove, or so it seemed, and busy towns grew up around them. Places like Fesserton, Waubashene and Victoria Harbour all owe their origins to the sawmill days. Port Powell would have too if it had gone anywhere. In 1846, its plan was laid out just to the west of present day

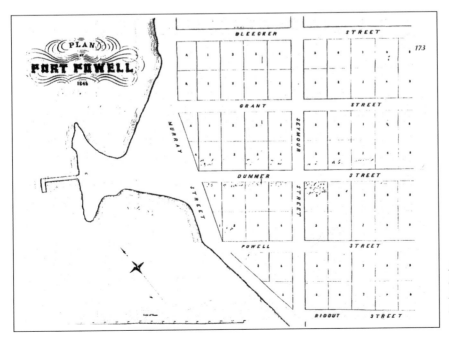

Port Powell never became the Georgian Bay milling town that its promoters had hoped.

77

While Franktown did attract some handsome and historic buildings, most of its village plot remained empty.

Victoria Harbour. Eight streets and nearly 100 housing lots were created around a wharf. However, the days of the lumber business were waning, and the harbour was not as reliable as the planners had counted on. Port Powell remained a forgotten paper town.

Only with the countryside sprawl that has engulfed rural Ontario in recent decades has the paper plan seen development.

Franktown

Many of Ontario's earliest town plans were military plans. These were created not so much for defense, but rather by the military for retiring officers. Even though hostilities had ended, it was never a bad idea to have some military types around, just in case. Near Ottawa, Richmond and Perth were laid out following the War of 1812 for the officers who had served in that conflict. A military road linked the two. Halfway along the planners created a third town, Franktown. A large townsite was laid out in 25 acre lots, and planners waited for the influx. It never came. While Perth and Richmond flourished, Franktown attracted only a handful of pioneer businesses — stores, taverns and churches.

While Franktown never really flourished, neither did it disappear. Many of its historic structures still stand, among them the stone St.

A few old structures yet linger on Waverley's old town plan.

James Anglican church and a hotel. However, long laneways and quiet side streets serve as reminders that the dream of becoming a grand town was never realized.

Waverley

As the Rocky Saugeen River tumbles westward through the hills of central Grey County, the rushing rapids attracted many mills. The mill sites gave rise to most of the towns that still flourish in the area today — and to others that never did. In 1856 surveyors Milton Schofield and Thomas Collier, believing that the pioneer frontier would soon sweep across the area, laid out a townsite that they called Waverley. Just to entice purchasers a little more, they added to their plan a few industries. That the so-called industries had not yet arrived didn't seem to matter much to the pair. Perhaps they had real hopes, or perhaps they were utter frauds. In any event, a sawmill and grist mill were soon in operation. A decade after their futile attempt at creating a real town, John Travers bought the plot and the mills and changed the name to Traverston, a name it goes by to this day.

Gradually the place grew into a typical pioneer community with a general store, blacksmith, and briefly, a woollen mill. But the town of which Schofield and Collier dreamed never materialized. Eventually

79

all the businesses closed and Traverston became a ghost town. Only the grist mill, which is now a house, and a few former shops cling to the roadside. The rushing Rocky Saugeen, however, has attracted a new breed: country dwellers who find the rushing river and its cedar-lined river banks an attractive environment in which to live.

Suckertown

Before roads were cut into the dark forests, Ontario's towns and villages clung to the mouths of creeks and rivers that protected the lake schooners, which were the life line of early Ontario. On the shores of Kettle Creek, upstream from Lake Erie, Captain Joseph Smith in 1840 laid out just such a town. He called it Selbourne, although locals insisted on calling it "Suckertown" after the fish that lazed in the muddy waters. (Some insisted that it referred to the people who bought lots in the place). For a time the port bustled with a hotel, two distilleries, stores, shops and mills alongside the wharfs and warehouses. But the place was plagued by floods. And later, when the London and Port Stanley Railway bypassed it and went directly to the lake, Selbourne died, and its town lots lay weedy and unclaimed. Meanwhile, just a short distance away, the village of Port Stanley sprang to life with a deeper harbour and railway connection. It remains a popular lakeside resort and busy port, and its railway now carries tourists.

Saxtontown

Shortly after Selbourne began to grow, John Saxton laid out a town of his own upstream on nearby Otter Creek. While a few lots were

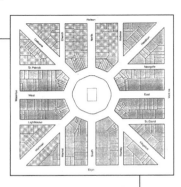

DESIGNING A TOWN

Only a few dared to try something different. John Galt gave to Goderich, at the terminus of the Huron Settlement Road, a radiating street plan that had been devised two thousand years earlier by a Roman town planner named Marcus Vitruvius. To this day it remains the world's best surviving example of a Vitruvius plan.

sold and a road surveyed, Port Burwell was better situated right on the lake to accommodate lake schooners, and Saxtontown quickly faded.

Jamestown

Like Saxton and Smith, James Chrysler dreamed of making it big in the land business. An American, Chrysler used his Yankee bravado to reap his riches from speculating in land around the boom town of St Thomas. He then turned his attention to the shores of Lake Erie where the hinterland remained cloaked in thick stands of profitable white pine. He decided that on the shores of Catfish Creek, a short distance upstream from Port Bruce, he could have it all: water-power, timber and a port town.

In 1835 he hired land surveyor Daniel Hanvey to lay out the valley into town lots. To get his cash flow going he then built a distillery, for in pioneer Ontario there could never be too much whisky. He then added the customary saw and grist mills, and warehouses where the scows could load up on timber for shipment from Port Bruce.

But the usually crafty Chrysler overlooked one important thing; every spring the snowmelt unleashed torrential floods that roared through the fledgling town and damaged the dams and often the mills. Little wonder few bought his town lots. And being too far upstream for schooners, the place could never be a port. The railways might have saved it, but they passed the entire area by in favour of Port Burwell to the west. Even the lucrative distillery could not withstand the onslaught of high taxes on booze. Then, once the timber was gone, Chrysler walked away and Jamestown sat empty.

Nearly all traces have vanished. Only the pilings in the river remained visible. Today a side road twists its way east of County Road 36 through the steep gully. Although a few modern homes have been built nearby, "Jamestown" remains a grassy floodplain on the banks of Catfish Creek.

Lockerby

In 1851, when Thomas Hembroff and David Lyons looked over their land in Elderslie Township, they smiled to themselves. They were confident that the Elora Settlement Road would pass right through it and boost its value tenfold, perhaps more. And so on the flat banks of the Saugeen River they laid out a townsite with 60 lots along a half dozen streets. Their hearts sank, however, when they learned that the Elora Road was to bypass their townsite and go through Paisley instead. In an attempt to salvage his investment, Hembroff built a grist mill. Attracted by the water power, others added sawmills and another grist mill. A few lots were taken up and a school built on one them. Although the roads and the rails came nowhere near Lockerby, the reliable flow of water, and the prosperity of the farmers nearby kept it a busy mill site until the 1960s when the last mill fell silent and then demolished to make way for a picnic ground. Picnickers in the conservation area today would never realize that the grassy field where their dogs run and their children play was once to have been an important town. At least in the eyes of the dreamers.

Oliphant

Power boats roar and bounce over the waves, swimmers ease tentatively into the chilly Lake Huron waters. In a way, Charles Rankin's 1851 Oliphant townsite did become a centre of activity. But not quite in the way he had envisioned. In Rankin's day, the islands that hovered offshore protected what many thought were a limitless supply of fish. On them, dozens of fishermen built their shanties and set forth in their mackinaws to reap the bounty. Confident that the fishing industry would prosper, Rankin laid out on the mainland 15 streets, with town and park lots along them. Unaware of how overfishing would destroy the stock, the fishermen had soon cleaned out the fish and Oliphant faltered, never becoming anything grander than a small, rural service centre. Then in the 1950s and '60s with the boom in cottaging and highway building, Oliphant found a new lease on life as a resort community. But it was, however, a century too late, and Rankin would never know the unexpected way in which his dream would come true.

Seldom Seen

Perhaps there was never a more fitting name for a town that would never be. But to landowners Robert McCormick, John Van Nostrand, and David Richardson, the location couldn't have been more promising. It was the 1860s and railway fever had gripped York County ever since Ontario's first steam engine puffed into nearby Aurora a decade before. Beside the mill site on the steep banks of a creek, the three laid out a townsite. But even for busy York County, the location was too remote and the town plot was dubbed "Seldom Seen", even by the railways. Although a branch of the Grand Trunk came temptingly close, the place never had more than a pair of sawmills. When these shut down, the name disappeared, even from the railway map. Then in 1926, the railway line itself was lifted. Today the housing development which has crept up the St. John Sideroad and McCowan Road has been halted by the steep banks of the gully, and in the words of local historians the old townsite remains "seldom seen."

Hoodstown

Railway fever struck the beautiful Muskoka country later than it did in southern Ontario. By the time the Northern and Pacific Junction Railway was finally pushing its rails through the unrelenting swamps and hard rocks of Muskoka in the 1870s, the area to the south was crisscrossed in a spider web of rail lines. But the effect was the same. Wherever the line appeared headed, land values skyrocketed.

In 1880 when Janet Hood registered a town plan of 40 acres, she was certain that at least one, and maybe two railways were coming her way. She wasn't alone. Within 10 years her town on the shore of Lake Vernon could claim three general stores, two churches and a hotel. Things looked so promising that in 1891 Charles Hood laid out another plan on the opposite side of the river.

But when neither railway reached town, the place stagnated, and one by one the businesses closed. The NPJ Railway had chosen Huntsville, Hoodstown's rival on the opposite side of the lake, while J.R. Booth built his Ottawa Arnprior and Parry Sound line several miles north. The Hoods' dreams lay shattered.

But Hoodstown had one thing going for it — its fabled Muskoka beauty. By the 1930s Toronto cottagers had discovered the natural charm of the area and began a cottage boom that endured well into the 1970s, when it was replaced by another building boom: rural sprawl. Today modern homes peak from the trees that have grown up on the old town plot. The Hoods were simply a hundred years too early.

Baldoon

Alexander Lord Selkirk is much better identified with the successful Red River settlement in Manitoba than he is with a failed scheme to settle Scottish Highlanders in southwestern Ontario's swamp lands.

Maybe it was the incentive of getting 150 acres for himself for every colonist he attracted (the colonists themselves got a mere 50 acres), or maybe it was the treeless expanse strategically situated by the St. Clair that drew him into this scheme. Whatever the attraction, Selkirk in 1802 ordered the land to be surveyed; small parcels for the settlers, and a 1200 acre estate for himself, all southwest of modern day Wallaceburg. The settlers would work for Selkirk's estate to pay him back for their land and for transporting them. Raising sheep was the mainstay of the colony.

In 1804 the first of the rugged Scots began arriving with their families. They spent a dismal winter huddled in 14 cramped log cabins. The autumn rains were relentless. Much of the land was inundated, and by spring, 16 settlers were dead from malaria. The following year brought renewed hope and more settlers arrived. However, wolves and rattlesnakes decimated the sheep flock — more than 300 died that winter alone — and overspending by Selkirk's manager threatened the scheme once more. The colonists themselves were described by the manager as "the most drunken, quarrelsome, and indolent of any people in Upper Canada".

By 1820, distressed by the costs and the mismanagement, the British Colonial Office declared the scheme a failure. The settlers dispersed and Selkirk himself died in April of that year, broken and exhausted.

Parts of the deadly swamp have now been filled to accommodate new development, sprawling outward from Wallaceburg.

St. Joseph

One of the most ambitious of Ontario's dreamers was Narcisse Cantin. Born on the shores of Lake Huron of French Canadian descent, he grew into an ambitious cattleman. His many trips to

Narcisse Cantin dreamed his St. Joseph would become a great city. But that hope was shattered when the government failed to build a canal to his site.

Buffalo showed him the enormous boom that a canal could bring to land values. Near his home he began to amass large tracts of land and hatched a scheme that he hoped would make him a millionaire: he would simply persuade the federal government to build a canal, one that would cut across Ontario's southwestern peninsula from Lake Erie to his own land on Lake Huron.

He laid more than two dozen streets and 400 lots and named his town St. Joseph. He enticed two dozen French Canadian families from their new homes in Michigan to return to Canada and settle in his town. His ability to persuade lured his Buffalo business buddies to set up industries there — a winery and a brick yard among them. He built a business district that included several shops and his grand three-storey Balmoral Hotel.

Unfortunately, the outbreak of the First World War, and a federal government scandal, combined to doom his plans. The canal never arrived, and neither did any more businesses. His hotel stood until 1928 but never once opened its doors. Today a historical plaque (on Highway 21 35 km south of Goderich) marks the site of the hotel and the failed dreams of Narcisse Cantin.

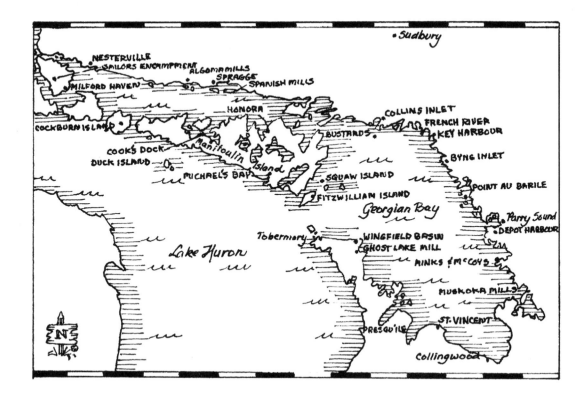

6

Ghosts of the Bay

——⁓☙☙⁓——

Before the industrial revolution swept urban Ontario, and before the railway age reached its zenith, Ontario's most industrialized shoreline was that of Georgian Bay. From Tobermory on the tip of the Bruce Peninsula, to the coves and islands of the North Channel, there were more than three dozen busy sawmill towns, and countless summer fishing villages. It was a time when the backshores of the bay were cloaked in thick forests of white pine, and the cold waters teamed with whitefish and lake trout. It was a time when the bounty seemed endless.

During the summer months, the sawmills hummed with activity. The mill hands cut the logs into boards for schooners to carry off to the growing towns and cities to the south. During the winter they trudged into the forests to cut more logs and pile them on the riverbanks for spring drives down the foaming rivers. Hundreds were crushed trying to free jammed logs. In 1897 the industry appeared headed for collapse when the United States passed the hated Dingley Tariff, blocking the import of manufactured lumber from Canada. Ontario fought back by banning the export to the U.S. of saw logs, a move which lured American sawmills into Canada.

The cold waters of the bay were also the fishing domain of a few large fish companies. Outfits with names like the Buffalo Fish Company, the Gauthier Company, the Booth Company of Chicago and later, the Dominion Fish Company, held licenses which divided the bay and northern Lake Huron into exclusive territories. These companies in turn hired or contracted individual fishermen to provide them with their catch. From April to August, the tiny islands and shoals close to the fishing banks found little harbours crowded with the skiffs and mackinaws that the fishermen used to venture into the often mountainous waves. Wintertime found them back in their home ports, caulking their boats or mending their nets.

The mill towns were rough and ready. The cabins and boarding houses where the hands lived, some with their families, were crude and drafty. If they were lucky some of the residents might enjoy the presence of a church or a school. A few even had the rare luxury of a doctor or a hospital. These were seldom needed on the fishing islands, places which were occupied usually only during the short fishing season.

Georgian Bay's heyday was doomed to be short-lived. By the end of the century the pine forests had been ripped down and many of the fishing grounds depleted by overfishing or destroyed by sawdust. But other changes were at work as well. As the remaining fishermen turned more and more to larger diesel and gas-powered tugs, they could reach their fishing grounds right from their home ports and the summer fishing villages became obsolete. Railway lines had begun to penetrate the northern woods, exposing more stands to the loggers' axe, and the mills relocated from bayside to railside.

Unlike the vanished villages of southern Ontario, there has been little to replace the mill towns and fishing villages of the bay. In a few places cottages have been built where mill towns and fishing villages stood. In most, however, the rocks and the remoteness have discouraged most such intrusions, and here the ghosts of the bay rest in peace.

Wingfield Basin

Wingfield Basin, at the tip of the Bruce Peninsula, was the centre of a small sawmilling industry and fishery. Most evidence of this activity has long vanished. However, one very visible ghost is the skeletal hull of a more recent wreck, that of the Gargantua in the 1950s. Of the earlier activities, however, only a few rotting timbers tell the tale of long ago. Located at the dead end of a narrow dirt road that follows the shore north from Dunks Bay beneath the towering cliffs of the Niagara Escarpment, Wingfield Basin offers a tranquillity almost unheard of in urban Ontario.

Ghost Lake Mill

Despite being the perfect name for a ghost sawmill village, the appellation predates the lumber days. Before Europeans colonized the

For the most part the once familiar scene of drying fishing nets has vanished forever from the islands of Georgian Bay, along with the villages of the fishermen.

region, a large number of native residents were ice fishing on the tiny mountaintop lake. A sudden wind shift caused the ice to crack and float far from shore. The terrified tribesmen looked on helplessly as the ice disintegrated beneath them and one by one they plunged to an icy death. Believing the site to be cursed the remaining villagers left the dreadful place calling it a ghost lake.

Undaunted by the spectre, lumberman Hiram Lymburner re-named it Gillies Lake and used it to float logs to its outlet at the brink of the Niagara Escarpment. From there he simply hurled them over the cliff to the mill pond below. To reduce the damage from the plunge, Lymburner cut a channel from the lake and built a water flume down the precipice.

Down below, the mill and the cluster of workers' hovels were crammed onto the narrow, bouldery beach between the cuesta and the tossing waters. There was no harbour here, and the location was often ravaged by the howling storms that raged out of the east. One such storm sent the lumber vessel the Nellie Sherwood to a watery grave. Or was it the curse of Ghost Lake.

It was no curse that had closed the mills by 1905, however; they were simply a victim of the short sighted practice of clearcutting. While nothing remains of the village at the base of the looming cliff,

89

the vestiges of the trench and the flume lie at the summit for those hardy enough to struggle their way up the cliff. It is about halfway along the road from Dunks Bay to Wingfield Basin.

Presqu'ile

Located north of Owen Sound, this little peninsula enjoyed a short-lived prosperity. During the 1860s and 1870s it was an important fuelling depot for the many steamers that plied the bay's perilous waters. In those days the steamers used wood, and the forests here were plentiful and close enough to allow the protected site to become a busy settlement. Donald MacKenzie laid a town plot that focused on the warehouse, store and lighthouse, and the community swelled to a population of 200. In one year alone (1878) nearly 350 vessels called for fuel. Eventually the lake steamers switched entirely to coal brought to Owen Sound by rail and the fuelling depot at Presqu'ile was no longer needed. Today it is a residential area consisting mostly of cottages or houses that dot the old streets.

St Vincent

Like Presqu'ile, St. Vincent, or Cape Rich as it was later called, was a fuelling depot for the steamers. With its small fishing fleet the little port, located east of Owen Sound, soon counted 100 residents on its small network of streets. Eventually the steamers stopped calling and the fish stopped biting, and the place became a ghost town. When the Canadian armed forces incorporated the site into its Meaford Tank Range, its buildings were used for target practice, making it one of the few ghost towns in Ontario to go from bust to "boom."

Muskoka Mills

The south shore of Georgian Bay is busier now than in its milling heyday. Although the railways and the industries have now come and gone, the area remains a tourist haven. Provincial parks and cottage developments line the shore, while ski slopes have slashed into the forested hills of the Niagara Escarpment, as onetime mill towns like Waubaushene, Victoria Harbour and Fesserton have found new life. But despite the cottage boom that has engulfed even the Thirty Thousand Islands, a few old mill ghosts repose quietly in the back bays and more remote channels.

In 1876 the Muskoka Milling and Lumber Company built at the mouth of the Muskosh River a large sawmill and about two dozen cabins for the millhands and their families. There was a school for their children to study in, and upstairs a church to worship in, while the Rossin House Hotel provided rooms for visitors to stay in.

Logs for the mill were either floated down the river, or boomed across the bay from the forests on the north shore. No matter where they came from the sawdust ended up at the bottom of the cove. Once the authorities realized that the dust was poisoning the fish spawning beds, they took the owners to court, an indication that there were some concerns over pollution even in these pre-environmental days. However, the suit was dismissed and the pollution continued. But the mill didn't last much beyond that. By 1895 it had shut down, a victim of its own over-cutting.

Time has taken its toll on the ghosts of Muskoka Mills. Accessible only by small motorboat or canoe, the cove contains only rotting lumber and some cribbing.

> A royal commission in 1898 discovered to no one's surprise that the very fishermen whose livelihood depended upon the fishery had for years been using undersized nets, and exceeding the amount of netting allowed. One estimate held that more than 2,000 miles of nets were strung in Georgian Bay at any one time. Pollution charges against mill operators whose effluent had decimated the fishing grounds were either enforced with only minor fines or dismissed outright.

The Minks And the McCoys

Many of the names of Georgian Bay's islands have become legends in their own right: the Westerns, the Limestones, the Pancakes, the Umbrellas, and the Minks and McCoys. Although these islands were barren and windswept, wherever a cove could shelter the wind-powered mackinaws of the fishermen, there was likely to be a fishing station. Such was the case on the latter three islands. The largest of these was that on the Minks. More than 150 residents huddled there, living in drafty shanties, as crates of fish sat on the wharf waiting for the fishing company's tug to call. The residents could enjoy few amenities. Besides the crude huts, the icehouses and the netsheds, there was only a small building that served as church and community centre. A cow provided milk while a "floating grocery store" called periodically with provisions.

By the 1930s fishing had changed on the bay and the last of the

Mink Island fisherman sailed away into the chill autumn breezes. Later on, cottagers moved into some of the larger shanties and converted them into summer homes. Here and there a crumbling shanty lies neglected, sagging a little bit with every year that passes.

The Umbrellas and the McCoys did not have large operations and for most of their history may have been the domain of a solitary operator. This may be one of those rare "ghost" sites that has a ghost. Some have said that every September, under the full moon, the ghost of "Big" McCoy, a trader who reputedly cheated his native clients, howls in agony just as it has every year since that September when, under a full moon long ago, he was mysteriously murdered.

Point au Barile

One of the Thirty Thousands' beauty spots, Pointe au Barile attracted a fishing colony and tourists as well. A string of small coves near the open waters harboured the fishermen's mackinaws and their simple shanties. A few shells from those days still stand vacant and deteriorating. On other islands nearby stood the resorts, the Belleview Hotel (now a ruin) and the magnificent wooden Ojibway Hotel, which has become a private non-profit club owned by the area's history-conscious cottagers. The most photogenic building is the centu-

Only a few shells from the early days survive at Pointe au Barile

ry-old lighthouse, now automated. Pointe au Barile Station is on Highway 69 and provides the easiest boat access to the location.

Byng Inlet

It was once the largest sawmill town on the bay north of Parry Sound. Here the Holland and Graves Lumber Company at its peak cut and shipped 20,000 board feet of lumber a day and was the second largest mill of its kind in Canada. On the south shore of the inlet (named after British Admiral Byng) stood the village with its hotel, church, school, dance hall, movie house and several streets of large houses. In 1927 the mill shut down and the residents moved away, some to the booming CPR coal dock town of Britt on the north shore of the inlet. Although Byng Inlet had acquired a railway station, it was some distance from the town, and with lumbering the area's only economic mainstay, it could do little to save the place. Located a short distance from Highway 69, the Inlet has bounced back a bit as a resort town and yet retains the old hotel, store, church and a small number of the mill workers' houses.

Key Harbour

Tucked into the northern-most corner of Georgian Bay, Key Harbour was an important port, at least for a while. Strangely, it began with the opening of a mine more than a 100 km north. The Moose Mountain mine near Sudbury shipped iron ore pellets via the newly constructed Canadian Northern Railway to boats waiting to carry it to the American foundries. But the cove proved too small for the larger boats that began to ply the lakes, and the CNo converted the docks to a coal harbour. A seven mile spur line led from the CNo main line at Key Junction where a railway village sprang up. Key Harbour could boast the wharfs, a powerhouse, boardinghouse, and several dwellings. Nearby were the shanties and icehouses of a fishing colony.

Arthur Gropp outfitted a Model T Ford to run on the rails and made a business of meeting hunters at the Junction, while hauling fish for the Gauthier fishing operations. By 1950 the CNR had converted from coal to diesel and closed the coal dock. Seven years later they abandoned the spur and lifted the rails.

French River's rocky terrain made it difficult to locate houses and roads alike.

Summertime still finds the remote place busy with cottagers and a few commercial fishermen. But the ghosts of its heyday lurk everywhere. The pilings from the wharf protrude from the waters, while submerged cribs urge boaters to be on their guard. On the shore the shell of the power house still stares across the waters. The right of way for the old spur line is now a snowmobile trail, while in the tall grasses near the onetime wharf lie the rusting wheels from the railway days. It is a long boat-ride from Highway 69 at Key River down the remarkably straight channel to the ghosts of the Key.

French River

One hundred years ago, the chimneys of the French River Mill so dominated the skyline that ships' captains used them as a guide to help them navigate through the tricky channels of the French River mouth. Yet of all the vanished mill towns around the shores of Georgian Bay, none so large has vanished so utterly as has the town of French River. During its heyday, from the late 1870s until 1912, great piles of cut lumber would often hide the village from sight.

The village consisted of two sections, old Wabbtown, the older section with the two churches, the school, and the shanties built by founder Sam Wabb, and "Copananing" the Ontario Lumber Company townsite, with its rows of look-alike houses perched high on the barren rocks. The three hotels did a brisk trade not just with the mill hands, but with the loggers and the commercial fishermen who inhabited the countless islands and back channels. At its busiest times the town contained nearly 1500 people.

Had the Canadian Northern Railway extended a spur line to the site, as it had to Key harbour, the town might have survived. Although the railway line runs right through Hartley Bay a short distance away, bridging the many channels put the cost beyond what even the ambitious McKenzie and Mann, the CNo's prolific promoters, were willing to pay. To compound matters, in 1912, lobbying by the influential Gauthier Fishery over pollution of the fish spawning beds paid off, and the government outlawed the dumping of sawdust. The lumber company declared bankruptcy, and within a few years the town had been dismantled leaving only foundations and debris, and a few sunken boilers. With its thick growth of brush, its broken terrain, poison ivy and rattlesnakes, it is a difficult place to visit. And the maze of channels render it difficult to even find without a proper navigation chart — now that the chimneys are no longer there to guide us.

Collins Inlet

French River's nearest neighbour was Collins Inlet. Another sawmill

The village and mill at Collins Inlet have been replaced with a fishing camp.

95

town, it burst into life in 1886 when John Bertram purchased a small mill, expanded it and added a townsite. While most mill hands lived in the boarding house, a few, who came with their families, occupied larger houses. When the mill burned in 1918, there was no point in rebuilding — most of the timber was gone anyway.

It is, however, a ghost town that has stood the test of time (better than French River, anyway). The boarding house stands yet, now a part of the Mahzenazing River Lodge (permission to visit is required). The foundations of the mill lurk in the bush, while pilings from the old wharf protrude from the water. And on the rocky shore overlooking the beauty of this remote and tranquil channel, stand a pair of forlorn and vacant houses.

The Bustards

Travellers venturing between French River Village and Collins Inlet see on the watery horizon the low profile of a series of islands. Windswept and remote, these are the Bustards, once the busiest summer fishing village in north Georgian Bay. The 559 islands and shoals which make up this island cluster also make the waters tricky to navigate. The fishermen used a straight, deep channel known as the "gun barrel" to reach their shanties where they piled crates of whitefish and lake trout for the Dominion Fish Company. The fishery lasted longer here than on many other islands, some families still fishing from the place until the 1950s. A few of the former fishermen's cabins are now summer cottages, although the distance and the shoals make it no easier to get to.

Squaw Island

One of the Bustards' main competitors was Squaw Island. Located well to the west of the Bustards, the colony at Squaw started in the late 1870s, and by 1900 had grown to 80 fishermen, many of whom brought their families with them. More than 45 "smacks" (boats) and 3 tugs were stationed here. As the local headquarters for the Buffalo Fish Company, they could enjoy the presence of a school and summer mission church. In a good season Squaw Island's fishermen would haul 10 to 15 tons of fish every week, mostly lake trout, whitefish and chub. But the good seasons didn't last long. By 1920, overfishing had reduced the stocks severely and that summer saw fewer than two dozen fishermen arrive. By the 1950s a new predator, the sea lamprey, had so decimated the remaining fish that the fishermen stopped coming altogether.

Fitzwilliam Island

Located just off the southeast point of Manitoulin Island, Rattlesnake Harbour on Fitzwilliam Island proved to be one of the more durable of the summer fishing villages. At the turn of the century it was the summer home for the families of more than two dozen fishermen. Across the little harbour on Jennie Island stood the icehouses, warehouses and the company store. While the number of fishermen using Fitzwilliam declined over the decades, the fishery hung on until the early 1960s. Even now, many dilapidated cabins still line the rocky shore, collapsing a little more into the water as each season passes.

Duck Island

Here the Gauthier Fishing Company kept three of their fishing tugs and by the turn of the century more than 100 people were calling the fishing colony their summer home. A sawmill was located here as well. When the mill closed in 1937, the fishermen had all gone, and the place became a ghost town. Today, other than a few bits of timber, there is little to indicate that there was anything here at all.

Cockburn Island

One of the most compelling of the ghosts of the Bay, Cockburn Island is a ghost island township, complete with reeve and council, yet with a permanent population of just three. Originally the site of a fishing station founded by Zeb Tholsma, the large island also attracted sawmills and about 40 farmers. The island soon became an organized township and Tholsmaville grew to be its administrative, social and economic centre. Steamers called regularly giving Cockburn Island a link with the outside. But as the timber supply shrank, and the fishery became depleted, the population dwindled from more than 300 before the First World War to fewer than 150 after the Second World War. Then, in the 1960s, the CPR discontinued the steamer service and the residents were forced to leave their homes, most moving to Manitoulin Island just to the east, or to communities on the North Shore. Few, however, gave up their love for the island or their family homes. While many buildings are now vacant, others are maintained for summer use, while among them a few new cottages have appeared.

Michaels Bay
Located on a now quiet cove on the south shore of Manitoulin Island, Michaels Bay had two reasons for being there. The shelter of the little cove meant that boats could safely call. Many of those early vessels brought the first settlers to this the largest freshwater island in the world. From the dock they followed the crude settlement roads through the forests northeasterly to Manitouwaning, and northwesterly to Gore Bay.

Others came for the lumber and Michaels Bay's sawmill became its economic mainstay. Powered by the flow of the Manitou River, it began operation in 1867 and by 1870 was turning out 10 million feet of pine lumber per year. By 1885 it could claim a population of 400, with stores, boarding houses, taverns and about 15 frame houses all located on the town plan devised for the site (although most builders paid scant heed to the lot line).

By the 1890s, however, its mill had closed, and many of its residents had moved away. Later, as South Baymouth — a short distance to the east — developed a fishing station and became the port of call for steamers (and now the large car ferries), Michaels Bay was abandoned entirely with no trace other than vague cellar holes.

Honora
The north coast of Manitoulin Island is one of Ontario's most scenic. Nestled into cliff-lined coves are some of Ontario's prettiest villages — places like Meldrum Bay, Gore Bay and Kagawong. It is also the site of some intriguing ghosts. The site of an early sawmill, Honora was laid out on a town plot in the 1890s and grew to include a grist mill, a fishery, and briefly, a brickyard. At its peak the mills turned out more than three quarters of Manitoulin's wood shingles, and was the island's largest shipper of timber. Although the mills and dock are long gone, the site remains an attractive residential community

and is 20 km west of Little Current.

Cook's Dock

To anyone travelling along Highway 540 as it skirts the shore of the North Channel, it would be hard to believe that this silent stretch of beach once contained a busy fishing station, a mill that turned out a third of the island's timber, and a wharf from which timber, hides and wool were regularly shipped. Once these operations closed there was nothing to keep Cook's Dock going and it was abandoned.

Spanish Mills

Located on Aird Island, just off the mouth of the Spanish River on Lake Huron's North Channel, Spanish Mills became one of the larger mill villages of the area. Millhands lived in the boarding house, or in one of the 20 little wooden cabins with their families. The place also contained a school, church and store. In 1927 the mill was moved to Skead, east of Sudbury, and Spanish Mills was abandoned. Today only a few piles of discarded lumber serve as reminders of its heyday.

The Stolen Sawmill

One of the aims of the Ontario government ban on the export of uncut logs to the United States was to encourage American mill owners to locate their mills on Ontario soil. Bart Moyles took that literally. In 1893 he stealthily disassembled his mill in Detour Michigan and floated it to John Island near Spanish Mills, minutes before the sheriff could catch up to him. The mill prospered in its new location with many businesses and a population of 300. In 1918 the mill burned and the town was abandoned. Today the site is the summer home to a troupe of boy scouts.

Spragge

The sign on Highway 17 announces a "Spragge" that seems to be alive enough. This is today's Spragge, a residential community strung along the highway. But the Spragge of yesterday isn't here; it is down by the water where, from 1873 until 1931, sawmills were the focus for a different sort of town. Operated by the Cook Brothers Lumber Company, the mills on the shore attracted a population of 250, while the "upper" town, clustered around the station of the Canadian Pacific Railway. In 1903 it became part of the vast MacFadden empire which included mills all along the North Shore, until 1931 when the company moved the operation to Blind River. While "upper" Spragge continues to thrive, thanks to its location first on the railway, then on the highway, the shore contains only the docks, the old streets and the mill foundations of another of the ghosts of the bay.

For many years the old hotel at Sailors' Encampment on St. Joseph Island sat empty.

Algoma Mills

What remains of this early mill town is also due to the CPR and Highway 17. But it has a unique claim to fame. In an attempt to build its early line to the West Coast through the United States the CPR began to lay tracks westerly from Sudbury to Sault Ste. Marie. Re-elected after an embarrassing defeat, Prime Minister John A. MacDonald reasserted the all-Canadian route and the CPR halted its line at Algoma Mills, thus making it for a brief period, the CPR's western terminus. The railway company built docks, warehouses, coaling facilities, and laid the foundations for a grand hotel. But with the re-establishment of the all-Canadian route, none of these were needed and the CPR abandoned them. Now the old road ducks under the railway bridge from Highway 17, south of the logging museum, and leads to the shore. Although all traces of the docks and warehouses have vanished, the stone foundations for the proposed grand hotel still hide in the woods.

Nesterville

Once the site of the Thessalon Lumber Company Mills, and just six kilometres west of the scenic community of Thessalon, Nesterville on MacBeth Bay consisted of two dozen houses clustered around the mills. Although the mill lasted only a couple of decades, many of the old village buildings remain standing, a few of them vacant. Others were obliterated when the Sault Ste. Marie Highway (now Highway 17) was built.

Sailors' Encampment

Here, on the west side of St. Joseph Island, Tudor Rains (yes, Mr. and Mrs. Rains named their son "Tudor") built three docks for steamers to stop and refuel. The place contained the Rainsmere Hotel — a rambling wooden hotel that became a popular tourist destination during the 1930s and 40s, the now restored Church of Mary, built in 1876, and the one-room log school that sits in the St. Joseph Island Museum complex. During the days of steamships, hopes ran so high for the fledgling town that T.N. Molesworth laid out an extensive town plot. However, when the steamers switched from wood to coal, they passed the place by and it became a quiet rural settlement. The unusual name came about from an early event when a vessel found itself frozen in and the sailors had to camp there for the winter.

Milford Haven

This sawmill town was created by William Rains, the founder of St. Joseph Island, to attract settlers from England. To sweeten the allure,

Depot Harbour's hotel was a busy place when John Booth's grain terminal provided grain shippers with their shortest route to the Atlantic.

101

he provided a store, mill and parcels of land for them. While the island attracted settlers and prospered, Milford Haven never matched Rains' expectations. The scenic little bay on the south shore of the island is attracting cottagers now, yet a number of the remains of the mill town still lurk behind the cover of a new forest.

Depot Harbour

The largest of the towns to become a Georgian Bay ghost, in fact the largest in all Ontario, was John Rudolphus Booth's Depot Harbour.

In 1866 Booth moved from his Waterloo Quebec farm and rented a mill in Ottawa. As the new kid on the block he stunned the Ottawa lumber establishment by using cheap labour to undercut their bids on the contract to supply lumber for Canada's new parliament buildings. He outfoxed them again a few years later when he won the rights to the pine rich Egan timber limits in Algonquin Park. In the meantime he had been busy assembling a network of rail lines that connected Ottawa with the Atlantic Ocean, the Canada Atlantic Railway. Booth never did things by halves. When he extended his rail network into the park to get at the logs, he kept on going. By wrestling a moribund railway charter from its Parry Sound proponents, he gained rail access to Georgian Bay. Rather than benefitting the town, as Parry Sound residents had hoped, Booth bypassed it and built an entirely new town on Parry Island, offshore from Parry Sound. That town was Depot Harbour.

Depot Harbour contained 110 houses on a dozen streets. The place also had three churches, a school, boarding house, the Islander Hotel, and several stores. But no booze. For fun and games the residents had to travel to a Parry Sound suburb named Codrington (by decree of founder William Beatty, Parry Sound was also dry), a boisterous hotbed of bars and bordellos which acquired the less-than-flattering nickname of "Parry Hoot".

Back in Depot Harbour, trains puffed in and out of town, sometimes as frequently as every 20 minutes. In the harbour, the best natural port on the Great Lakes, steamers glided up to the massive grain elevators, discharging their cargo of wheat from Duluth.

Depot Harbour had become one of the busiest ports on Georgian Bay. But it wasn't to last. By 1920 the Canadian National Railway had taken over the railway and the town, and shut down its facilities there. A decade later, when ice damaged a trestle in Algonquin Park, they didn't bother to repair it. Depot Harbour suddenly was without a reason to exist and the grain elevators sat empty. Then, during World War II, the Chemical Industries Limited (C-I-L) explosives plant at nearby Nobel used the elevators to store the highly volatile chemical cordite. When the War in the Pacific ended in August of 1945, local celebrants lit a victory bonfire on the docks. But a gust of wind blew the flames to the elevators, and the repository erupted in a midnight fireball that illuminated the streets of Parry Sound, 10 km away.

Ten years later the houses were sold for just $25 each and the lumber hauled away to become cottages, garages and outhouses. Today the massive railway roundhouse, roofless and crumbling, guards the road access to the place. Behind it are the overgrown rail yards, and the sidewalks and foundations of the townsite. Down by the dock sit the ruins of the office vault, still firmly in place, and the rusting relics of an iron pellet shipping operation that was Depot Harbour's only activity in its later years. From the rocky knoll where the Catholic Church once stood, the visitor can hear in the chilly wind that blows in off the tossing waters the wailing chorus of the ghosts of Georgian Bay.

With few other amenities to enjoy, the residents of Depot Harbour would gather at the general store. Only ghosts remain.

103

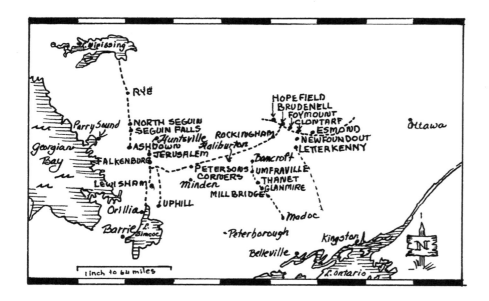

7

The Great Colonization Road Scheme

F ree land! It seemed too good to be true, and it was. Yet this was the lure that drew thousands of unsuspecting land-hungry settlers to a dreary wilderness of rock and swamp between Ottawa and Georgian Bay during the 1850s and 1860s. It was a time when the lush farmlands south of the Canadian Shield were full, and yet immigrants were looking for more.

But it was also a time when Ontario's (it was called Canada West at this time) lumber companies were looking further afield. The forests of Southern Ontario had been cleared as had the great pine stands of the Ottawa Valley. But in the tortured rocks and dismal swamps that lay west of the Ottawa Valley, the pine stands stood thick and untouched. The only problem was that no settlers lived nearby. Essential to the lumber camps, the settlers provided a source of men with strong backs willing to earn good money toiling in the winter bush camps, of horses to pull the logs to the frozen rivers to ready them for the spring drives, and of potatoes and meat to feed the hungry loggers.

To fill the void, Peter Vankoughnet, the Minister of Agriculture, devised a scheme that on the surface seemed philanthropic and humane, yet under the surface was callous and conniving. The scheme was to build a series of "colonization roads". They would number more than 25, and along them the land would be free. The owner needed only to build a house and put 18 acres under cultivation. While the government propaganda touted the fertility of the soil, the surveyors were warning that the soil was so poor and rocky that it could scarcely grip their survey stakes.

The first to open was the Opeongo Road, a tough pioneer track that twisted through the Black Donald Mountains from the Ottawa River to Opeongo

Lake. It was followed by others with names like the Addington Road, the Hastings Road, the Peterson Road, the Victoria Road, the Muskoka Road, and, the last of the lot, the Nipissing Road.

And the hopeful settlers came by the thousands. Walking, hauling wagons, or crammed onto jolting stages, they made their way into the unknown wilderness. Along the way was the welcoming sight of stopping places, crude cabins that passed for hotels, where the pioneer settlers would overnight on route to their promised land. Many of these hotel sites grew into villages. Other villages clustered around the few mill sites to be found in this unrelenting land.

Then the scheme began to unravel. The lumber companies razed the forests and left. A few years of productive crop yields were about all the sandy soils would give to the pioneers. Cleared of the forests, the rains washed away the light soils, and the farms turned into rocky wastes. Roads agents wrote of terrible hardships and even starvation in their reports, and the embittered settlers fled. The farms became wastelands of weeds and scrub forests, and the villages stood silent. These are the ghosts of the roads of broken dreams.

> **CORDUROY ROADS**
>
> Some of the early roads were planked with logs laid side by side (corduroy), but most were merely cleared paths.
>
> Ontario would have to wait until 1915 for its first concrete intercity road, which ran between Toronto and Hamilton (at the time one of the longest such roads in the world).

THE OPEONGO ROAD

The easterly portion of the Opeongo Road passes a lowland of relatively good land. Followed now by Highway 132, the Opeongo's farms have been replaced by rural subdivisions and unsightly strip development. But then the road hits the looming rock wall of the Black Donald Mountains. As it twists its way through the mountains, it retains many of the early pioneer cabins, barns and the vestiges of villages that were once far busier than they are now.

Esmonde

Other than the St. Joseph's Catholic church two and a half kilometres west of Highway 41, and the one-time schoolhouse, nothing remains of the pioneer settlement of Esmonde. One of the few fertile sections of this length of the road, it grew into a busy community. But with the decline in the number of farmers even here, it dwindled to nearly nothing.

106

Newfoundout

About one kilometre west of Esmonde, a narrow dirt trail leads up the side of the mountain. It is the road that once led to the colony of Newfoundout. High on the rocky plateau a band of hopeful settlers carved their farms from the forests. Over a stretch of about three miles of road, the colony numbered a dozen farms. There was no village although a post office used the name. Children had to make their way down the steep hill to the school below. But the harsh land and the isolation drove most away, and the place was utterly abandoned. Today the forests have begun to reclaim the fields, and many of the old log cabins and barns have collapsed into mounds of rubble.

Clontarf

Hemmed in by brooding peaks, Clontarf was for the settlers a busy rural community with a church, store and hotels. Of the older buildings, some log farm homes and a church remain. Further along, the road begins its steady climb up the rocky heights and passes one of the road's historic sites; the Raycroft and the Plauts Hotel, pioneer stopping places, are both now private homes. The St. Clements church was built in the 1850s.

Clearing the way, whether for road or railway construction, this scene was typical in 19th century Ontario. Here, a team of men and horses clear the land for a railway line.

107

Foymount

Decidedly out of place on this pioneer path is this post World War II radar base. Having outlived its role in the early 1970s to warn of onrushing Soviet missiles, it was abandoned. Cloaking the highest peak in the mountains were curving streets, large houses and several blocks of apartments. Many of the base buildings have new tenants, others lie vacant. Although most of the houses are occupied, the apartments yet lie empty. A short distance east, in utter contrast to the modern base, is the Vanbrugh log school that served children of the pioneer community from which the base took its name.

Brudenell

It was of the busiest stopping places on the upper Opeongo. Here were houses, stores, a pair of lusty hotels run by the Costellos and the Payettes, and a disapproving church. The old Costello Hotel was said to be a haven for gambling and other sins. It stands yet, now weathered, beside the old store. A small village cabin across the road also bears close scrutiny. A short distance west the large brick Catholic church which once closed its eyes to the shenanigans nearby, still stands, confident that those days are long gone. Brudenell's size and relative prosperity was due in part to its strategic location at the intersection of the Opeongo with another colonization road, the Peterson.

The rough and tumble Costello Hotel in Brudenell still stands as a private home.

108

Hopefield

The focus of this rural community west of Brudenell was its sawmill and stopping place. The rugged house that once was filled with loggers and pioneer settlers is now a private home. West of Hopefield the Opeongo Road joins Highway 60 at the busy tourist town of Barrys Bay.

THE HASTINGS ROAD

This road was surveyed about the same time as the Opeongo and was intended to join the latter at Opeongo lake. Neither road made it that far. With its southern starting point at Madoc, the Hastings Road wound through a terrible land of low rocky hillocks and interminable swamps. Only here and there were small patches of soil large enough to sustain the small pioneer farms. Of all the colonization roads, it fell the furthest. Of the 400 farm lots originally granted, by 1925 a mere 75 remained occupied. In walking the road in that year, retired surveyor C.F. Aylesworth lamented that all that remained of the settlements were "empty dilapidated abandoned houses and barns and old broken down fences." Today there are fewer than a dozen, although many of the old farm lots now sprout newer country homes.

> **IN THE NAME OF PROGRESS**
>
> "The Ottawa and Huron tract is known to contain a large amount of arable land...there is no portion of Canada which can offer the same inducements to industrious immigrants," wrote Thomas Keefer. Government officials, especially Peter Vankoughnet, agricultural minister, felt that this section of Ontario could accommodate more than eight million people. What area was he referring to? Algonquin Park.

Millbridge

On land granted to Captain Ralph Norman, as a reward from the British for his service in the Crimean War, the town enjoyed one of the better water-power sites on the Hastings Road. Not surprisingly, it became one of its larger communities, where a fall fair became a festive occasion for farmers from many miles around. It could boast a school, church, the mills and a hotel that was nicknamed "Cupids" for reasons that can only be imagined. Only a few of the original buildings, the school, a store and community hall among them, have survived, and most are now used for different purposes. They lie about 30 km north of Madoc, just west of Highway 62.

Glanmire

The next mill site north of Millbridge, Glanmire was originally called Jelly's Rapids after an early settler. While it existed it contained a hotel, store and church. The last to crumble was the place of worship and today only a cemetery remains.

Thanet

Beyond Glanmire the road traveller would arrive at Thanet. Another of the stopping places, it contained a school, church, mill, and three hotels, including the well known Thwaites Place. Again, only the cemetery remains.

Umfraville

North of Ormsby, a road community that has managed to survive, Umfraville grew to include Jorman's Mills, Spurrs' Store, a church, school and a few other village enterprises. Besides the now weedy mill pond, and a few older houses, there is nothing to indicate that a busy pioneer village once existed here.

Beyond Umfraville the road links with Highway 60 and the roadside development that lines it from there into Bancroft. North of this bustling town, Highway 60 continues to usurp the old Hastings Road's right of way and none of the pioneer elements have survived the relentless strip development that now plagues what was once a scenic and historic route.

THE PETERSON ROAD

At least half of the Peterson Road no longer exists, nor is it even traceable. It was one of only three of the 25 roads to run in an east-west direction and linked Brudenell on the Opeongo with Muskoka Falls near Bracebridge on the Muskoka Road. Few settlers took up land along it and villages were far between.

Rockingham

The most interesting of the lot is Rockingham, about 15 km east of Combermere. With the lonely board and batten pioneer church that overlooked the townsite, it has dwindled markedly since pioneer times. Although it retains many other pioneer era buildings, it could be considered neither vanished nor ghostly.

Petersons Corners

It was a different story with Petersons Corners, however. Located where the Peterson crossed the Bobcaygeon Road, it was a crossroads hamlet with store, post office and hotel and a few log shanties. Nothing has remained from those pioneer times.

THE ADDINGTON ROAD

Letterkenny

Although Highway 41 has taken over most of the right of way, a few back trails remain on forgotten portions of this route. North of Denbigh, long segments are abandoned, indeed some were never opened. However, near its intersection with the Peterson Road, just east of Rockingham, sits the wooden Letterkenny church — the only survivor, aside from a few farms, of that historic rural settlement.

THE VICTORIA ROAD

Uphill

This route, now Highway 505, began its lonely journey northward at Victoria Road on what is now Highway 48. After crossing the dry

Although there were no hills to speak of at Uphill, it marked the start to the Victoria Road, where most of the land was so terrible for farming, that the route is now largely abandoned.

limestone plains of Victoria County, the road peters out. The only place to recall those early times is Uphill. Of most of the buildings that clustered about the intersection, the hotel, store and most of the houses have gone. Only a church, now minus its bell tower, and a couple of older houses mix with some newer nondescript buildings.

THE MUSKOKA ROAD

Lewisham
Probably the liveliest of the old trails, the Muskoka Road is now known as Highway 11 and is a four-lane, limited access road to cottage country. No ghosts here. To find the vanished villages it is necessary to venture on down the side roads. One place along an abandoned side road is Lewisham. In the heart of Ryde township, or what used to be called that, along a now little-used trail that leads southeast from Coopers Falls, it consisted of a store, church, and school and was a scattered and hard-pressed community of bush farmers. After the Second World War just about everyone had left and the road fell into disuse, and remains that way.

Falkenburg
North of Bracebridge as the Muskoka Road bent to the northeast, the Parry Sound Road branched northwesterly carrying settlers to Georgian Bay. At this important junction the village of Falkenburg grew. With its log church, store and two hotels, it was a popular gathering place for local farmers, as well as being a vital stopping place. But in the 1890s the line of the Northern and Pacific Junction Railway, later the Grand Trunk (now CN) passed nearby, and the station village quickly outgrew the road village. Later, as new roads bypassed the old intersection, the site of Falkenburg became a backwater, and most of its old buildings disappeared. Today a few new homes occupy some of the original 50 lots, the only original vestige being the pioneer cemetery. The Parry Sound Road has become Highway 118, while the Muskoka Road, at this point, simply disappears into the woods.

Jerusalem
It was common in pioneer Ontario for settlers to name their com-

munities after places in the Bible. And the handful of hardy pioneers who had followed Thomas Peacock up the Muskoka Road north from Bracebridge were no exception. In a pleasant valley just beyond the turbulent north branch of the Muskoka River, they carved out a clearing and erected eight log homes. As the years passed, the community was abandoned and only a pair of log buildings still stand. The site lies in a field surrounded by forest, north of High Falls and west of Highway 11.

THE NIPISSING ROAD

This was a late comer. Even as many of the earlier colonization roads were facing ruin, the Nipissing Road in 1875 began to feel the boots of its first settlers. They could disembark from steamers at Rosseau on Lake Rosseau and follow the new route from Ashdown, on the Parry Sound Road, as far north as Lake Nipissing, a trip of several days. Stopping places were located at six-mile intervals, the distance that a struggling team of horses could journey in a half day. The pockets of tillable soil were few and far between. Nor were any larger cities nearby to cushion the failed farming and lumber economy. Most of the stopping places and villages have vanished or contain little more than a few ghostly relics of the optimistic times when new settlers saw it as a road of fresh hopes.

Crumbling cabins tell the sad tales of colonization road hardships. This one lies on the Nipissing Road.

The King George Hotel. Now gone, was once a busy stopping place for Nipissing Road travellers and Booth line rail trippers alike.

Ashdown

This was the jumping-off point for Nipissing Road settlers and occupied the junction of that road with another busy colonization road, that which led to Parry Sound. In its heyday of the 1870s and 1880s the crossroads could claim a store, church, Orange Lodge, carriage factory, blacksmith and the hotel run by the pioneer Ashdown family. By the 1900s the railways had made their way into the area, and Ashdown lost even its post office. Only the cemetery has survived from those days.

Seguin Falls

There are two locations for this interesting ghost town. When the road first opened to travellers, Seguin Falls was a small stopping place at a crossroads north of what is today Highway 518, with Burk's Hotel, a church, sawmills and Fitzer's store and post office. Two decades later J.R. Booth's railway surveyors laid the tracks of the Ottawa Arnprior and Parry Sound Railway a few kilometres south and Seguin Falls moved to trackside and boomed. A new hotel, the King George, opened beside the station, and the community grew to include a pair of stores, and about 20 houses and cabins lining the road. Seguin Falls outlasted the other stopping places along the Nipissing. But once CN abandoned the line in 1958 the place dwindled until in the 1960s, Toronto Telegram travel writer, Harvey Currel was able to call it a "ghost town worth visiting". Not much has changed in Seguin Falls since Currel wrote those words. The old hotel has burned and one or two of the old houses have been fixed up. While it may not be as "ghostly" as it once was, it is still a piece of history that is worth a look.

North Seguin And Dufferin Bridge

Located within a mile of each other these two places had between them an Orange Hall, church, sawmill, blacksmith, carpenter, Vigras' store and the Plumtree Hotel, although all these buildings are now nothing more than cellar holes.

Rye

It's getting harder and harder to find Rye these days. The road north of Magnetawan was less travelled than the portion south of it. And that is the case even today. While Magnetawan is a busy little tourist town, and the Nipissing Road south of it wide and gravelled, and in parts even paved, that to the north remains narrow, winding and dark, much as the early travellers might remember. In fact several sections have been abandoned altogether. About 20 km north of Magnetawan, sat Rye. With its neighbouring village of Mecunoma, it contained a church, school, store and four hotels, including the widely known "Bummers' Roost". While a couple of old structures still stand precariously at Mecunoma, the site of Rye is now just a few fields of rubble. The last building to stand was the church and the original Bummers' Roost was replaced by a later building.

Horseless Carriage

In 1898 Hamilton businessman, John Moodie brought a one-cylinder "horseless carriage" into Canada. In 1907, the Ford assembly plant at Windsor had been one year in operation, and there were 2,131 registered car owners in Canada. By 1930 that number had grown to more than 1.62 million.

The Nipissing came to an end at the village of Nipissing on the lake of the same name. Just before that, in the hamlet of Commanda, the Gurd Historical Society has preserved the elegant general store as a living museum, a delightful reminder of the way things were when the settlers were making their way up this road of broken dreams.

8

Whistlestops

They were once the lifeline of every small town and village in Ontario. They were the link to the outside, and a community's very survival depended upon them. They were, of course, the railways. Ontario's first railway was a horsedrawn affair that in 1835 struggled up the Niagara Escarpment near Queenston and linked Niagara-on-the-Lake with Chippewa above the thundering falls. It is Aurora, however, that claims Ontario's first steam railway connection. In 1853 the citizens of what was then called Machel's Corners gathered around a wooden, shed-like station to watch the Ontario Simcoe and Huron Railway's little steam engine puff and wheeze to a halt.

Within half a century southern Ontario would be crisscrossed with a spider web of rail lines and would be part of a rail network linking the country from coast to coast. Communities that had been days apart by horse or stage were now just hours away from each other. Products could now be hauled by tons in the wooden boxcars, rather than by the mere cartload in the back of a horse-drawn wagon, and trackside factories replaced the village craftsmen.

The railways changed forever the very face of a province, and communities lobbied hard to get one or more if they could. Some, once friendly, became bitter rivals when competing for a rail line. Those that succeeded boomed into prosperous industrial towns. Those that failed became ghost towns.

Some communities simply hadn't existed at all before the trains came along. These are the places created by the railways — the station villages — enabling the railways to run. Here stood the station with its vital order board, a water tank, coal dock, freight shed, and livestock pens. Behind the station a typical hotel would await travelling preachers and businessmen, while busier stations might even boast a restaurant. And around them grew the railway settlements.

The railway created three types of settlements: the new town, the satellite

John Booth's station in Douglas has been gone for many years.

town and the whistlestop. Railway companies would take it upon themselves to build entire communities when given the land to do so. Using town plans from their plan books, they laid out a grid network of streets, with the main street typically ending at the back door of the station. This way, arriving travellers would see, before anything else, a wide and bustling main street, while shoppers would see the station at the head of the shopping street and be constantly reminded of the dominance of the railways over their very lives. While this was commonplace in the prairies where towns just didn't exist before the railway arrived, it was less so in Ontario where many villages were in place before the Rail Age.

At times railways shunned these existing towns. Seeking the cheapest land, the railways often located their facilities some distance away and literally made the town come to them. Here were the satellite towns. Often duplicating the name of the original town and simply adding the word "Station" to the end, some actually outgrew the parent town.

Then there were the whistlestops. These were the places along the line that needed minimal facilities and where trains would stop only when required. If a station agent was needed at all, he was usually a part-time or caretaker agent. Otherwise, aside from the coal dock, water tank, and freight facilities, there was little else.

The fates suffered by these three kinds of places have varied. Some have been gobbled up by sprawling towns and cities, some have become silent backwaters, others have vanished utterly, leaving, if lucky, only a name on some old maps.

The decline began in the 1930s. By then the Canadian National Railway had been created by the federal government to run the many smaller lines that the War and overbuilding had bankrupted. These included even the staid and steady Grand Trunk Railway and the upstart and overambitious Canadian Northern Railway, the line pieced together by the entrepreneurial duo of William McKenzie and Donald Mann.

The first major line to go was the MacKenzie and Mann's Canadian Northern line from Toronto to Ottawa. For a time Ontarians could choose to travel between Toronto and Ottawa or Toronto and Montreal on one of three main lines: the Grand Trunk, the Canadian Pacific and the Canadian Northern, all leading east from Toronto, all servicing the same lakeshore communities. In some locations the lines were so close to each other that train engineers were literally within shouting distance. By the forties most of the track was lifted. The towns that it served were among the most prosperous in Ontario, and most continued to be. The CN and CP still called and, after the war, they would be linked by Ontario's most ambitious highway, the 401.

However, many of the little CNo's satellite villages and whistle stops fell by the wayside and became relics, or ghosts, or vanished altogether.

The next major line to go was the colourful old "Booth Line Railway". A hundred years ago, John Rudolphus Booth was Canada's richest man. He got that way by undercutting the Ottawa lumber establishment in the 1860s to land the lucrative contract to supply lumber for Canada's new parliament buildings. He struck again a few years later when he grabbed away the rich pine stands in Algonquin Park. To reach them, however, he needed a railway. And so he built one, an extension of a network of lines he had already assembled in eastern Canada by the name of the Canada and Atlantic Railway.

But by using the name the Ottawa Arnprior and Parry Sound, he acquired more government grants, took over an inactive charter from a Parry Sound consortium, and pushed a railway across the uninhabited wilderness that stretched between Ottawa and Georgian Bay. Villages appeared instantly at railside, and beside the waters of the bay, he built a brand new grain port, Depot Harbour.

Apart from the grain and the lumber, the line generated little revenue and in 1904 he sold it to the Grand Trunk at a loss of $4 million. When the CN took it over in 1923, the line was more than the new railway giant needed. In 1933 when ice damaged a trestle in Algonquin Park, the CN didn't even bother to repair it, severing the once busy route. By the end of the Second World War the track had disappeared west of Scotia Junction, the line's link with the CN's main line from Toronto to North Bay. However, trains still puffed eastward from Scotia Junction into the park carrying tourists to the wilderness lodges until 1958, and then these rails too vanished. East of the park, sections of line were lifted bit by bit, and now Booth's once glorious route consists only of a short spur line to Renfrew. Most of the villages that had depended entirely upon the trains have vanished as well; a few have survived as tourist or retirement centres, while Depot Harbour went on to become Ontario's most extensive ghost town.

After the war, encouraged by car and tire manufacturers, the Ontario government went on a wild road-building spree and killed the many rail lines that linked Ontario together. Colourful local lines that had provided seniors and students with their only means

The Grand Trunk's Joe Lake station was built of logs to help attract tourists to this Algonquin Park locale.

120

The attractive little Crosby station was evidently being used as a home while the line of the Brockville and Westport railway was seeing less and less traffic.

of getting around fell silent: the Bay of Quinte Railway from Deseronto to Bannockburn, the Irondale Bancroft and Ottawa from Kinmount to Bancroft, the Central Ontario from Bancroft to Trenton, the Grand Junction from Belleville to Peterborough, the infamous Rice Lake Railway, defeated ultimately by yearly ice jams on Rice Lake, the Midland Railway that linked Port Hope with Midland, the Victoria, the Nipissing, the Hamilton and Northwestern, and the ambitious Sarnia branch of the Canada Southern, all disappeared from the landscape. Even the CPR, southern Ontario's only private railway to survive unscathed, closed historic branch lines that it deemed to be less than profitable: the Pontypool and Beaverton, the Georgian Bay and Seaboard, the Ontario and Quebec, and even portions of the historic Credit Valley and Toronto Grey and Bruce lines, all fell victim to the CPR's corporate bottom line.

And all along these lines are the vanished villages and whistlestops that will never again relive the railway age. No longer will they hear the distant whistle, or the squealing iron wheels, or experience the bustle and excitement of passengers hurrying on and off the coaches, hugging long-lost friends and family, and waving that last good-bye from the coach window as the train edges away from the platform.

Now preserved on a private lot, the COR's historic Bronson Station was a simple whistlestop.

These are the ghosts of the railways.

Bronson

When the Central Ontario Railway was being planned, its promoters had hoped to link with John Booth's railway, which would pass to the north. In the short term, however, it would simply tap the iron deposits further south. But the mines were short-lived, and the dream of linking with Booth's line thwarted. Trains usually did not go beyond the large station at Maynooth. Passenger service ended in the 1960s and the tracks were lifted in the 1980s. Today this historic route is a snowmobile trail, with a string of vanished villages en route.

Bronson pre-dated Bancroft and served as the headquarters for the Bronson Lumber Company. When Bancroft began to develop around a mill site, Bronson's operations moved there. The flag stop station was relocated to a private yard on Highway 62 a short distance north of Bancroft.

Graphite and Hybla

The hills around Bancroft now draw rock hounds from across North America to crawl the crevices for rare and attractive stones like graphite, sodalite, and amazonite. But a century ago these rocks were valued for their industrial uses and spawned dozens of tiny mining camps. Most of the minerals were shipped through the stations at Hybla and Graphite. It's hard to see "ghosts" at either, for Hybla has become a rural settlement with newer homes lining the old railway line, while evidence of Graphite has vanished.

Millbridge Station

This is one of the more interesting of the vanished COR whistle stops. The station stop for the larger community of Millbridge, a colonization road "ghost", about four kilometres to the west, Millbridge Station still boasts its old brick "Hogans" station hotel, with hand-painted sign, an anomaly on a bush trail into the middle of the woods. It lies east of Highway 62 on the Stony Settlement Road. There is, however, no evidence of the station.

Wallace

For a short time Wallace was the end of the line and had a bunkhouse, store and church. Trains, however, seldom traveled beyond Lake St Peter, and most usually terminated at Maynooth. While the station still stands in Maynooth, there was no such structure at Wallace. Even the right of way is difficult to discern.

Algonquin Park

Created in 1893 as a national park, this is now Ontario's premier wilderness tourist destination. Today however, they arrive by car. But until 1958, most arrived on a train hauled by puffing steam locomotives. They disembarked at Algonquin Park station to stay at the Highland Inn beside the station, or at one of several other lodges that the Grand Trunk Railway had built throughout the park. The Ontario government has obliterated nearly all traces of this historic location. The hotel and station were demolished and the grounds planted with pine. Only the most determined explorer will locate the station platform near a ministry staff parking lot just off Highway 60.

Brule Lake

One of many Booth Line ghost towns in Algonquin Park, Brule Lake boasted a sawmill, boarding house and several family cabins. Algonquin Park hikers or canoers will still be able to see the clearing and the odd bit of metal or lumber from this vanished village.

Rock Lake

Formerly the site of the McCrea Lumber Company Mills, and the Booth family's remarkable Barclay Estate, Rock Lake contained a small, wooden station, a water tank, and a small collection of railway houses. After 1933, when the bridge over a nearby creek was destroyed, it marked the western limit of trains arriving from the east. Today all traces of the community have been replaced with a camp ground.

Douglas

Two kilometres south of town, a station satellite village contains only a pair of dwellings, one of them vacant, and the empty and weedy station ground. The parent village of Douglas, on Highway 60 west of Renfrew, still survives and retains a pair of oldtime lumbermen's hotels.

Scotia

The site of the most attractive station on the line, a decorative turreted building, Scotia was the Booth Line's junction with the Grand Trunk's North Bay route. Grand Trunk passengers would change trains here for passage west to Depot Harbour, or east to Algonquin Park. In addition to the station there was a water tank and several sidings. The original station burned in 1914 and was replaced by a simpler structure. After the Booth Line was lifted, the station was demol-

The Grand Trunk built several hotels in Algonquin Park, but none grander than the Highland Inn at Algonquin Park Station.

HIGHLAND INN, ALGONQUIN PARK, ONT.

At the junction of the Booth line with the Northern and Pacific Junction, the Scotia station was crowned with an attractive turret.

ished and the sidings removed. A few Railway Age buildings mingle with newer houses on Highway 592 south of Emsdale. The passenger trains of the Ontario Northland still speed past, but travellers looking out the window will see only fields where coaches, boxcars, and steam engines once sat on the sidings.

Seguin Falls

Of all the towns along the Booth Line, Seguin Falls fell the hardest. Originally a stopping place on the Nipissing Colonization Road, the businesses moved to trackside when the Booth Line was built. Here beside a shed-sized station, clustered the King George Hotel, a store, sawmill, school, church and a dozen or so cabins for mill workers. South of the track a tree-lined main street shaded the larger houses of management. When the rail was lifted in 1955, most moved away. While the hotel has burned, a handful of houses (most occupied only seasonally) and the former school still stand by the old right of way. It lies south of Highway 518 on the Nipissing Road, east of Parry Sound.

Swords

The community began life as a lumber siding for the Sheppard Lumber Company. But as tourists began to patronize the line, the

A simple worker's cabin still stands at Seguin Falls .

name changed to Maple Lake Station, and became a popular stop for wilderness seekers. While newer homes now dot the area, the old, weathered store, and a few vacant Railway Era houses give Swords a ghostly aura. It lies south of Highway 518 on the Swords Road.

Whitehall

Although Whitehall predated the Booth Line, it had only a post office and a "population" of 25. But the railway changed all that. By 1906 it could claim a general store, four saw and lumber mills, and a casket factory. With the end of the train service, the mills vanished and the store closed. Today, while a few residents still live in the area, the store sits vacant and the station ground has become the playground for snowmobilers.

Irondale

The Irondale Bancroft and Ottawa was another of those resource lines. It never reached Ottawa, nor did it build any grand stations. It did, however, leave a legacy much remembered by those who lived on the line, or who worked for it. But it also left a string of vanished villages in its wake. Irondale was once a busy iron mining town, its deposits the rationale for the early construction of the line. Today, the only remains of that community are the church and a few foundations along the network of dusty streets.

Many of the houses at Swords were no bigger than this.

Furnace Falls

This whistlestop was created to accommodate a siding to the nearby iron mines. But the mines had closed by 1900 and the siding removed. The place also had a shed-sized flag station and a freight siding.

Maxwells

This was the location of a small whistle stop east of Irondale on the IB&O Railway. The little shed-sized station survived the demise of the railway by 35 years but has since vanished.

Howland Junction

Named after local mining magnate L.R. Howland, this was the junction of the Victoria Railway with the Irondale Bancroft & Ottawa. A turntable, a two-storey station and a number of houses stood here. At the end of the Howland Road, east of Highway 121, the little flag station which replaced the earlier structure and a couple of houses still survive. In the bush lies the pit from the hand-operated turntable. While the Victoria Railway roadbed is now a snowmobile trail, the IB&O roadbed is overgrown and barely visible.

TORONTO'S LOST RAILWAY VILLAGES

Few of us within the mega-city of Toronto, and its sprawling suburbs, are aware that many of the historic communities within it owe their origins to the railway. For many decades, the waterfront area of

127

Toronto served as a hub for more than a half dozen railway lines that stabbed out in all directions. Along those lines lay whistle-stops, station villages and even major railway towns that have since been gobbled up by the city's relentless expansion.

Mimico

Now a neighbourhood within greater Toronto, Mimico began life as a station village. Here, by the tracks of the Great Western Railway, a grid network of streets was laid out. They contained the usual array of station village buildings (like the workers' homes), a small main street of shops, a trackside hotel and a station, as well as a railway YMCA. The extension of streetcar service and the improvement of the highways brought the village within Toronto's shadow, and soon it became part of the urban area itself.

Despite this, much of the old village can still be seen. The main street, Mimico Avenue, still contains a row of one-time stores, many of them now used for different purposes. Station Street still leads to the tracks and the site of the first station. Although now empty, Mimico's third railway station stands west of this site. However, the station hotel occupies its original location. Sadly, however, the railway Y, like most across Canada, has gone.

A church dates from Mimico's railway days

A string of workers' homes in New Toronto.

New Toronto

In 1891 Mimico got a new neighbour. In that year the Grand Trunk Railway opened extensive new yards a short distance west. Beside them a new town was laid out and industries began to arrive. Using once more the typical grid pattern of streets, New Toronto's planners numbered rather than named them. That legacy remains to this day with the roads numbered 1 through 39 east to west. While many of the streets still contain the workers' houses of the railway days, most of the industries have closed and the yards are now home to VIA Rail and GO Transit

West Toronto

The "Junction", as it is still called, was originally the conjunction of three railway lines—the Grand Trunk, the Credit Valley and the Ontario and Quebec Railways. The area boomed from being a stopping place and Dundas Street, the main thoroughfare, attracted stores, businesses and more than 30 real estate offices. Several handsome homes were built along the side streets, and many, like the Heintzman House on Annette Street still survive. The same cannot be said for the area's railway heritage. Despite the energetic efforts of local heritage proponents, the old village has lost its tudoresque CPR station and its

129

West Toronto's main residential street was Annette Street.

historic roundhouse, while the Grand Trunk station and the pedestrian bridge over the tracks are threatened.

After the arrival of streetcar service, West Toronto was taken over by Toronto's urban expansion. Were it not for the great pride "Junction" residents still take in their "lost" village, it would be hard to distinguish it from the urban area that surrounds it.

East Toronto

Many visitors and residents alike puzzle at the presence in the far east end of Toronto, of a "Main Street", seemingly so far from the present city centre. It was, however, the "main street" of a railway town called East Toronto. In 1883 the expanding Grand Trunk Railway needed new sorting yards and here, surrounded by farmland, they built them. The town which was laid out beside them contained workers' homes, stores, municipal offices, coal and lumber yards, a railway YMCA, and a main street called "Main Street".

The municipality remained separate from the City of Toronto until the 1920s when the city finally arrived. Many of these early landmarks have long gone. The Ted Reeve arena now occupies the site of the Y, the former police station is now a community facility, while the yards

Railway-era shops in East Toronto.

and station have been removed, in their place a small GO Transit commuter station. Many of the original workers' homes, however, still line Gerrard Street, although Danforth Avenue has replaced Main Street as the neighbourhood's "main street".

Leaside

Again, it may surprise many to learn that this upscale residential neighbourhood also owes its existence to a long-forgotten railway company. Shortly after the turn of the century, a pair of enterprising railroaders named William McKenzie and Donald Mann were piecing together a nation-wide railway network known as the Canadian Northern Railway. Two of the missing pieces were main lines from Toronto to Ottawa and Toronto northward. To anchor these lines, they needed a railway town.

Here, on the north side of the CPR's Ontario and Quebec line, they brought in their town planners to lay out a town. Built to resemble their showpiece, Mount Royal, which they had recently laid out in Montreal, Leaside contained curving streets, and a town centre, as well as the more functional yards and shops.

However, within a few years the railway was bankrupt and, like the Grand Trunk, became part of the Canadian National Railway net-

The railway engine shops show Leaside's railway heritage.

work. As Leaside's residential area began to develop, the role of the railway diminished and today is a little-known legacy of the area. Indeed, only a pair of Canadian Northern buildings survive. Amid an extensive area of more modern industry, the engine shops and the building that for a time served as a yard station, stand on Essendar Street.

Scarborough Junction

Like Mimico, Scarborough Junction was a railway village. In 1856 the Grand Trunk Railway laid its track through the area, establishing a station at Scarborough Village a short distance east. Then, in 1873, when the Nipissing Railway was built from Toronto to Coboconk, it established a junction at this location. The two-storey wooden station was built in a pattern identical to many along the line which still stand at Kirkfield, Victoria Road and Coboconk. The Scarborough station, however, burned in 1960.

Many of the community's earliest buildings appeared when it was a busy junction of two main roads known as Bell's Corners, now known as St. Clair and Kennedy. When the Junction was started, a new plan of streets was laid with names like Laurel and Linden.

During the 1950s and 60s the suburban boom enveloped the area.

The core of Scarborough Junction still has early buildings.

St. Clair was widened, the early buildings were removed and along the side streets new homes filled in the spaces between the old.

Today a new GO commuter station stands on the south side of St. Clair, while a few pre-fab railway shacks mark the site of the junction station. Some railway-era buildings can still be found along Linden and Laurel, but aside from that the railway village of Scarborough Junction is hard to identify.

Meanwhile, Scarborough Village, situated northwest of today's Markham Road and Eglinton Avenue, has long lost any railway function. Yet it still retains the network of streets laid out when the building of the Grand Trunk station led to land speculation. Amid the newer homes that moved in during the last few decades, a couple of earlier homes still linger from those heady days of rail.

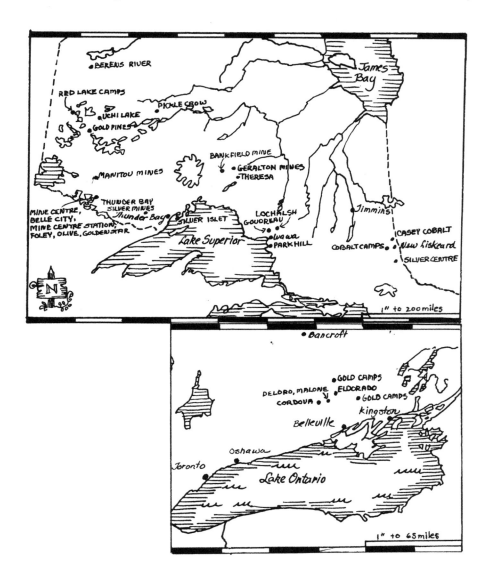

9

Gold Seekers and Silver Linings

Gold! Perhaps no word stirs men to action more than this one. Its very utterance has prompted stampedes, boom towns and murder. The dream of discovering golden nuggets has cost many men their fortunes, some their lives.

Ontario has a long history of gold and silver rushes. The earliest golden stampede occurred in eastern Ontario, a few miles north of Belleville in 1867. The latest, Hemlo, took place on the north shore of Lake Superior, east of Marathon, more than one hundred years later. In between were the silver rushes to Cobalt and the lakehead, and the gold rushes to the Porcupine, Kirkland Lake, the Seine, Gold Rock, Wawa, Longlac and Red Lake.

Mining camps were built atop the deposits. These usually were little more than the most rudimentary bunkhouses, cookeries, and maybe a few houses for management. Where the deposits were especially large, and where processing was needed at the site as well, townsites were laid out and often included schools and recreation facilities. One ghost camp had its own bowling alley and swimming pool and has them to this day.

Amidst the camps grew the boom towns. These provided the miners' needs what the camps lacked: hotels, pool rooms, cinemas, as well as bars and bordellos.

But when the deposit was depleted, camps and boom towns alike were left to wither and often disappear altogether. These are the ghosts of the gold and the silver rushes.

IN SEARCH OF ELDORADO

"On the 15th of August, 1866, I discovered gold." These words by prospector Marcus Powell would ignite Ontario's first gold rush, one that saw more than a dozen mines begin operation, and boom towns burst onto the rocky landscape. This was not northern Ontario, but near the Lake Ontario town of Belleville. But it didn't happen all at once. In fact it wasn't until two months after Powell's discovery that the local newspaper, the Madoc Mercury, let the word out. Rumours outraced the prospectors, some telling of nuggets that weighed more than 20 pounds.

But the winter of '66 had frozen the gold fields solid. Finally, with the warming winds of spring, the rush began. Before that time only one stage ran between Belleville on the Grand Trunk Railway and Madoc, the nearest place to the gold fields. But as the snow melted and the ground thawed, four more were pressed into service. Crude wagons, they were crowded with all manner of miners, prospectors and speculators. Stopping places like the San Francisco Halfway House at Kellar's Bridge appeared almost overnight.

It was a field day for the charlatans — like the land speculators who advertised thousands of acres of "gold fields" for sale, or the self-proclaimed experts who published books like the "Gold Seekers Handbook" and the "Gold Hunter's Guide". But how much gold was there? Some newspaper reporters told of being shown deep shafts and rich gold samples, but no gold actually in place. Others told of sacks of ore being taken to the gold mills — ore that was laced with gold from somewhere else. The purpose of the ruse was to increase the value of otherwise worthless claims. Tensions increased between

Ingenious prospectors would often rig sails to their canoes as they searched for gold.

136

"mine" owners and the prospectors, and the government hurriedly assembled a force of 25 Mounted Police under Sergeant-Major Foxton, based in Madoc. They didn't have to wait long to be called into action. On May 1, 1867, prospectors in Eldorado began to grumble about the truth of the claims. Led by Barkerville veteran Cariboo Cameron, 200 of them marched on the offices of the Richardson Mine and confronted manager Seth Hardin. There they demanded to see the gold or else they would pull down Hardin's office about him. Satisfied at what they saw, the crowd dispersed. By the time Foxton and his Mounties showed up, they had returned to their hotels.

But the mine they saw was one of the few that yielded gold. Of 300 shafts sunk, only one third showed any gold. Other rushes followed in the 1870s and the 1890s but fewer than 30 discoveries were worth the effort of beginning a mine operation. Most were scattered over a wide area, and the mines consisted of bunkhouses, cookeries and the buildings needed for the extraction. Among them were three boom towns: Deloro, Cordova and Eldorado.

Eldorado

A name that evokes the lost city of gold in South America, Eldorado was laid out by surveyor C.F. Aylesworth and consisted of 126 lots. Within weeks the place boomed from a single cabin to more than 80 buildings. As long as the Richardson Mine produced, Eldorado prospered. And the Richardson was pulling out gold at $130 per ton. But by the 1870s the mines were running dry and Eldorado had become a ghost town, its buildings empty and weathered. But it didn't die altogether. The Central Ontario Railway put one of its little stations there, and the growing community of farmers that surrounded it kept it alive as a farm service town.

Today a number of its old boom town buildings still survive on Highway 62, including a trio of former hotels, onetime stores and some simple, weathered cabins. The Richardson mine is long overgrown, its shafts nearly invisible in the shrubs and only a few stone foundations are left of the old mill.

Deloro

Spanish for "Golden", Deloro boomed later than Eldorado. Of more than two dozen shafts sunk in the area, eight became producing mines under the Canada Consolidated Mining company. However, a high concentration of mispickel (a common mineral) in the ore meant the gold could only be extracted using the complicated cyanide separation process. Despite the difficulties, the mines managed to yield up more than 13 thousand ounces of gold by the First World War. For years after, Deloro processed cobalt from a reduction plant that used ore shipped from Cobalt. Deloro has become a quiet residential hamlet that can only reflect upon its glory days as a golden boom town. The areas of the old mines have been cleared, the grounds contaminated by the cyanide used in the milling process.

Cordova

Of the gold field boom towns, Cordova was the most prosperous. Not burdened with the problem of mispickel that had plagued the Deloro mines, its operations by the 1920s had produced more than 22,000 ounces of gold, as well as large quantities of silver. Like Deloro, it is just a ghost of its glory years, and still contains stores and houses that recall its boom times.

Malone

The smallest of the golden boom towns, Malone could claim fewer than a half dozen mines, and these yielded only a few hundred ounces of gold. The place had other functions to perform however, and was a busy stop on the Central Ontario Railway, shipping lumber and farm products. Most vestiges of both its mining and railway era have gone, and the place today is little more than a rural settlement.

THE GOLD CAMPS

Gold lurks yet in the hills of Hastings. At the ends of the old mining roads (now overgrown trails) lie places like the Golden Fleece Mine, northeast of the present-day village of Flinton, which between 1881 and 1921 produced nearly 500 ounces of gold. There were the Sophia and the Craig Mines, northeast of Bannockburn which produced about the same. Further east, in the county of Frontenac, were the Star of the East and Ore Chimney Mines. While the former managed to yield about 130 ounces in 1905 to 1906, the Ore Chimney produced nothing except a memorable quote from one disgruntled investor who thought the name appropriate, for there he could see his money "going up in smoke". Yet of all the mining camps it has retained the most remnants, including the shells of a powerhouse and mill, and until recently, the skeletal shell of the headframe.

Most of these forgotten camps have tailings and the rotting lumber of the camp buildings. Shafts, if not fenced, are a menace hiding in a new forest. Most are private property and some, like the Ore Chimney, are fenced off to bar trespassers. But because the process of gold extraction was not perfect, many pieces of ore were tossed into the heap with traces of gold yet in them. While worth nothing commercially, they remain a tantalizing lure for latter day "prospectors" who long to cry "gold!"

Michipicoten Gold

Although it has only been open to car traffic in the last 30 years, the Michipicoten area of Superior's northeastern shore is steeped in history. For two centuries its fur-trading posts guarded the gateway to the Missinaibi fur route, the north's busiest. Then as the 19th century drew to a close, Francis Hector Clergue began his empire based on the area's iron deposits. But the Michipicoten area also experienced not one, but two gold rushes. Overshadowed by the more massive iron operations, and long abandoned, they have been forgotten by time.

It was in 1897 when native trapper William Teddy brought a curious stone to the Michipicoten mission. To Teddy's delight it proved to be gold and the stampede began. From the steamer dock near the mission the gold seekers followed a rough wagon road to the shores of Wawa Lake where a crude town was beginning to take shape. A town plot was laid out and named Wawa. Many of its lots were quickly gobbled up by land speculators. By the mission another group of speculators had laid out the grandly named Michipicoten City.

While two mines, the Norwalk and the Grace, showed promise, the bubble soon burst, and by 1906 Wawa stood empty, save for a caretaker. But the gold was out there. With the discoveries at the Porcupine and Kirkland Lake fresh in their minds, the prospectors showed up again in the 1920s. This time the boom lasted longer. More than two dozen mines were opened, and a handful of towns burst into life to serve them.

Parkhill

Tucked into the hills that separate Wawa from the Michipicoten River, Parkhill served several mines: the Minto, the Darwin and the Parkhill itself among them. At its peak Parkhill was shipping $10,000 worth of gold a month, and discovering ore as rich as $40,000 per ton. The place boasted a hotel, poolroom, stores, churches, a jail, and several houses. Finally, when the mines were depleted, the buildings were demolished, or moved along the rough trail and reassembled in Wawa.

Goudreau

The place began life in 1912 as a stop on the Algoma Central Railway. When the Cline Mine began yielding its golden bounties in the 1920s, Goudreau grew into a community of 200. A large two-storey station stood by the tracks, while a store, church and several cabins lined the twisting roads. When the sawmill town of Dubreauville was created after the Second World War, logging prolonged its life. Even now, with new gold prospects being developed, a few residents still live in this partial ghost town.

Lochalsh

The tracks of the CPR wound through woods a few miles east of Goudreau, and a stop called Lochalsh became the jumping-off point for prospectors. It consisted of a few hotels, a station, and houses for the railway workers. While it died with the gold rush, the train still stops here for the summer residents who now use some of the old boom-time buildings as their summer camps.

GOLD ON RED LAKE

Until the 1920s Red Lake was just another remote northern lake, far from the nearest railway line, and home only to a pair of Hudson's Bay Company fur traders. Distance did not discourage prospectors and in 1922 silver was discovered on the rocky shores of the lake. But it did discourage investors, and it was not until Lorne Howey, three years later, uncovered gold and muttered the understatement, "Looks like we found it," that the mine promoters began to take notice.

Despite the fact that the entire area was frozen solid in January of

The Darwin mine was one of the Wawa fields' leading producers.

1926, the rush began. Few could have realized how difficult it was to get there. The jumping-off point was the railway town of Hudson, west of Sioux Lookout. Here the prospectors crowded every available room, and even slept on the floor of the station. The platform became a tangle of harnesses and yapping sled dogs.

As with any rush, boom-times meant boom prices. Some shippers charged as much as $14 a bag for flour, and $100 to ship it. By comparison the $11 the CNR charged to ship a sled dog by train seemed cheap. While talk swirled around Ottawa over whether to build a railway to the gold fields, nothing happened, and the route remained an arduous mix of lakes, rivers and portages.

But the gold finds were so spectacular that the passage was but a minor obstacle. Word of discoveries like the "golden sidewalk" just served to drive the gold seekers that much harder.

The route took them northeasterly from Hudson, and across Lac Seul, one of the largest lakes in northwestern Ontario. The lake came to an abrupt end at the English River where a Hudson's Bay post named Pine Ridge stood. From there a series of portages lead to East Bay on Red Lake where another boom town was beginning, a town that would become the still busy community of Red Lake. There, around the shores of the lake, 15 mines sprang into production which

141

over several decades, would yield gold worth $350 million. Another seven mines on nearby Woman Lake would produce $700,000.

From there the search went wider: more gold on Confederation Lake where the Uchi Mine sprang into production, on Cassumit Lake, and on Jackson Lake. Prospectors also turned their eyes north- easterly to more prospects on Sturgeon Lake and Pickle Lake where the tiny Root River "Railway" relieved the long portage to the mines (and was used exclusively for this purpose).

The successes of the mines varied. Some produced spectacular results for several decades, others lasted only a few years. Today most of the mines have fallen silent, their remains making for ghostly images. A few continue to provide the area with jobs and prosperity.

Goldpines

This small Hudson's Bay fur-trading-post-turned-tent-city was strategically located at a key portage between Lac Seul and the English River route to Red Lake. By late winter of 1926 the shores contained a store, bank, hotel, and jail, all under canvas. By summer, most had been replaced with permanent buildings of wood and included Kert's Store, an Imperial Bank of Commerce, three hotels and the jail. Just

The CPR station at Wabigoon was the jump off point for the Manitou Gold Fields.

out of view of the two constables was a combination, bar/bordello/ gambling den with the intimidating name "Bucket of Blood".

Known first as Pine Ridge, when the community applied for a post office, Ottawa responded that there already was such a post office, and the name became Goldpines. And Goldpines it remained, neighbouring the shantytown of Whiskey Flats until the winds of change began to fly against her.

The Red Lake rush was the first to use aircraft, and when flights began direct runs to Red Lake, the portage settlement was no longer needed. By 1933 Goldpines was a ghost town. News of its death proved premature, however, for in 1938 when a mine far to the east named Uchi Lake opened for business, Goldpines became an important air terminal. Planes departed minutes apart carrying men and equipment to the fledgling new mine, and for a few glorious months it was officially the busiest air terminal in the world.

But by 1945 the Uchi Mine had shut down. Two years later the Red Lake Road (now Highway 105) was opened from the railway to the south and the businesses that had been at Goldpines moved out to the new town of Ear Falls on the highway. Goldpines once more fell silent. Following its abandonment, the Ontario Department of Lands and Forests moved a forestry station into some of the old buildings, while a tourist lodge opened using others. Today it remains a pleasant place on the shores of Lac Seul, although the ghosts of is glory days, when it was the key community on the Red Lake gold rush route, are never far away.

Uchi Lake

In 1938, a road was punched through the woods from Goldpines to the shores of Confederation Lake. Here the promising mine of Uchi Lake was ready to begin operation. The townsite contained a hotel with bank and barber, and apartments and homes for the mine workers. Nearby on the shores of Confederation Lake, a community of shacks called Lost Bay, with its popular "Halfway House", catered to the miners' more "basic" needs. But the mine closed after just four years. The buildings stood vacant, and the road deteriorated. Many of the structures, including the hotel, have been demolished or have simply collapsed.

Berens River

More than 100 km north of Red Lake, Berens River (and remote communities like it) needed amenities. That is why this mining camp could boast both a swimming pool and a bowling alley. When gold was discovered here near the shores of South Trout Lake in 1935, the only way in was by air. However, heavy machinery could not be loaded into the aircraft of the day and the only solution lay in a road through Manitoba. Who would pay for the road? Not Ontario, for the road lay in another province, and not Manitoba, for the mine and the royalties belonged to Ontario.

Eventually a road did wind through the remote northern woods and the townsite grew to 210 workers and a total population of more than 600. There were houses for families and bunkhouses for single workers. It had its own school and power plant. But despite the time and money spent on bringing men and machines to the site, the mine lasted only a few years after, closing finally in 1948.

In the half century that has passed, it has changed little. Although many of the buildings have collapsed with age, and others were removed after it closed, the site of Ontario's remotest gold camp has remained alone with its ghosts, and its swimming pool and bowling alley.

THE RED LAKE CAMPS

Red Lake is a vibrant community, modern and growing. But today's activity is only partly due to its mines; the rest is tourism and servicing. While the two largest mining towns, Cocheneour and Balmertown (these names no longer legally exist, together they are the township of Golden) still depend on the golden depths, other nearby camps have closed and become silent ghosts, only partly occupied if at all.

The Starrat Olsen mine operated between 1940 and 1963, producing over $2.5 million dollars in gold. Close by was the Madsen mine, which brought up gold worth $82 million, while the second oldest of the Red Lake camps, that on MacKenzie Island, lasted 30 years (1935 — 1965) and yielded $22 million. While all the townsites that surrounded them still have occupants, the mines are silent ghosts.

Pickle Crow

Among the gold camps of the Pickle Lake gold field, three stood out above the rest. They were the Central Patricia, Pickle Lake and Pickle Crow. While the former two continue to endure a periodic boom and bust cycle, depending upon the vagaries of the gold market, Pickle Crow has gone for good. Yet in the beginning it was the largest of the three. By 1938 the townspeople could gaze out the windows of their white, wooden bungalows and see 100 more just like them along a one-kilometre stretch of road. Reflecting the wages of the day, the residents paid a mere $12 a month in rent. The mine was one of the field's wealthier, producing $32 million in gold in its 30 years. Then in 1966 the gold ran out, and the mine closed. But rather than try to use the houses for other residents, the Ontario Ministry of Natural Resources simply burned them down.

THE SEINE RIVER RUSH

Many Ontarians have not even heard of the Seine River. Fewer still know about the frenzied gold rush that once overwhelmed its shores. In the 1880s, the new CPR gave prospectors an opportunity to explore northwestern Ontario's rocky wilds. From Rat Portage,

Mine Centre's roads and buildings alike were rough and ready — much like its residents.

145

today's Kenora, they worked their way southwards taking steamers along the Rainy River to the creeks and streams that flowed into Rainy Lake.

A decade before the CPR began rolling through the area, gold was discovered on Hay Island in the Lake of the Woods. But it took the arrival of the CPR to bring the gold seekers and the miners in any numbers. The Sultana was the best of the lot on the Lake of the Woods. Shafts were constructed on at least seven levels, and the buildings consisted of a headframe, mill and a number of dwellings as well as the bunkhouses and cookery for the employers. Before it closed in the early 1900s it had produced a million dollars worth of gold. A couple of others, the Mikado and the Regina, together yielded a half million. Today only the rubble from the tailings remains and cottagers and boaters now roar through the same waters where stately steamers once carried the gold seekers with their dreams of wealth.

Mine Centre

Around the shores of Shoal Lake and on the Seine River, a dozen busy gold camps sprang up with optimistic names like the Gold Bug the Lucky Coon, and the Money Maker. In their midst stood the boom town of Mine Centre, the cultural centre for the rugged miners. Here, on a narrow peninsula that jutted into the lake, they could find a drug store, barber, tailor, restaurant, customs houses and jail. Three hotels, The Randolph, The Rutlidge and The Mine Centre were at the heart of it all. After drinking such brands as Mikado Pale Ale or Sultana Lager, they would waste little time in deciding who was the best fighter. Among their more colourfully named characters were Pegleg, Rattlesnake Bill and Chief Neverwash.

Down by the wharf the steamers the Majestic, the Maple Leaf and the Seagull kept the miners in contact with Fort Frances on Rainy Lake.

By 1903 the tiny deposits were exhausted and the mining camps closed. A couple of years later the rails of the Canadian Northern Railway were laid a few miles north, and Mine Centre was abandoned. A townsite was laid out by the new station and took the name of the defunct boom town. The Mine Centre Hotel was disassembled and barged to Fort Frances where it was reassembled as the Irwin Hotel.

Following the demise of Mine Centre the mining town, Mine Centre the station a short distance away flourished.

Mine Centre Station

Even though Mine Centre was fast fading when Mine Centre Station appeared, the latter too has become at least a partial ghost town. When the railway surveyors set down their transoms, they laid out a townsite here with the typical grid pattern of streets that railway planners so favoured. A single-storey wooden station stood on the north side of the tracks, while on the south side stores lined the main street and small, wooden houses sat on the rear streets.

In the late fifties, when the railway switched from steam to diesel, the need for stations like that at Mine Centre ended. The opening of Highway 11 in the mid-1960s meant that residents no longer needed to rely on the train to escape. Businesses moved out to the highway, where the newer homes were being built. The old townsite became a ghost town. In the 1970s a number of weathered and empty buildings still stood by the tracks, while the station had been replaced by a converted passenger coach. Now, however, even these are gone, and weeds sprout on the village lots.

Belle City

Mine Centre had a rival, Belle City. Laid out on the shoreline a short distance east, the place never matched Mine Centre. Even at its peak it had little more than a sawmill, a school, a handful of houses, and

This was typical of the many gold camps that surrounded Ontario's first golden boom town, Eldorado.

the usual hotel. When the rush faded, so did Belle City. But if this city never grew large, others among the Shoal Lake "cities" were never more than just paper towns: Seine City, Turtle City, and the plan by Chief Neverwash: Chief City. None of them had a chance to develop before the boom faded.

Foley
Another of the Shoal Lake mines, the Foley mine began production in 1893 and within three years had yielded $40,000 worth of gold. With its store, hotel, school and dozen or so miners' cabins, Foley was the largest of the gold camps. It died with the rest of them, yet a couple of the old camp buildings managed to last into the 1970s as summer camps for local cottagers.

Olive
Located on Little Turtle Lake, north of Shoal Lake, the Olive yielded little gold and closed around 1900. It reopened briefly in the 1930s but was no more successful than it was the first time around. A number of artifacts remain on the site including the rubble from the shaft and an ore cart.

The Golden Star
The most prolific of the Shoal Lake mines, the Golden Star located near Mine Centre managed to produce nearly 12,000 ounces of gold worth $165,000, and lasted until 1941. Little evidence survives despite this.

THE LONGLAC GOLD RUSH

By the 1920s and '30s gold rushes no longer resembled the frenzied mob scenes that accompanied the Eldorado or the Klondike rushes. Prospectors were grubstaked by large mining concerns, rather than simply in chase of a wild dream. Tom Johnson and Bob Wells were two such dedicated workers when in 1931 they discovered gold near Little Longlac. When he first laid eyes on the golden pay dirt, Johnson understated the discovery as he told Wells: "I thought we had something of importance". That "something of importance" would lead to the development of a half dozen busy gold mines and the creation of the town of Geraldton. Some of those mines, with their little townsites, and containing the ghosts of their glory days, have become part of this growing community. Others, however, sit silent in the regenerating forests.

Bankfield

Three years after it started producing in 1934, Bankfield added a 100 ton mill to its community of 35 houses on curving streets. Adjacent to it were the smaller Tombill and Magnet mines. A rough and muddy trail connected the mines with Geraldton 16 km to the east. On June 12, 1937, 125 guests travelled along it to see the pouring of the first gold brick, and the beginning of an era in this part of northern Ontario. After a brief shut-down during the War, Bankfield bounced back to life but lasted only until 1947. Over that decade the mine yielded 66,000 ounces of gold and 7,500 ounces of silver, and a considerable amount of community spirit. Old photos show ten young men proudly posing in the sweaters of the Bankfield Millionaires hockey team. But when the town vanished, all that remained were the photos. In 1952 the buildings were removed, and today travellers on Highway 11 can speed past the forest that hides those old streets, without once realizing that just a few metres away they hide the ghosts of a once busy mining town.

Theresa

The Longlac gold field was wider than anyone who was there in the beginning could have believed. Several miles east, near the lumber town of Longlac, Moses Fisher discovered more gold. Here in 1934,

A wagon load of silver sits unguarded on the platform of the Cobalt Station.

on the banks of the Making Ground River, the Theresa Mine sputtered to life in 1938, producing only 15 ounces of gold. In 1939 the company deepened the shafts and in 1946 added a 100 ton mill, and then deepened the shaft even more to 1,000 feet. Twenty workers' homes lined a half dozen village streets while a short distance away were the larger homes of management. But the Theresa was another of those short-lived gold mines, as so many were, and shut down in 1953 after yielding a mere 4,700 ounces of gold. Today the streets are overgrown, and rubble marks the site of most of the homes. Only a couple of the more substantial management houses remain occupied.

Geraldton

Three mines and their townsites hovered around the outskirts of Geraldton. The largest was the MacLeod Cockshutt Mine. The longest and the richest of the Little Longlac Mines, it operated from 1933 to 1963 and yielded 1.5 million ounces of gold, an equivalent of more than 2,000 gold bricks. The empty structures lie on the south side of Highway 11, at the entrance to Geraldton.

A little further down the road to the south lies the small townsite and the empty buildings of the Hardrock mine. With 160 men on the force, it closed in 1951 after producing 269,000 ounces of gold. While the townsite, only a half dozen houses, still has residents, the mine buildings that haven't been removed sit empty.

Geraldton itself began life as the railway access to the mines, and grew on a grid of streets by the station. Despite the collapse of the mines, the town has thrived and has now grown to encompass the old mining townsites.

THE MANITOU GOLD RUSH

Far from the nearest road, on the shores of the Manitou Lakes, sits one of Ontario's most haunting ghost towns. Now almost completely hidden by the young forest are the headframes, mills and cabins of a half dozen gold mines, and the remains of the boom town that served them — Gold Rock. It all began around 1898, when prospectors returning from the disappointing Klondike rush (disappointing for those who arrived there too late) hopped off the fledgling CPR at Wabigoon and fanned out to hammer at the rocky shores. The golden flecks showed up frequently on the Manitou Lakes, and several mines began operations. The greatest concentrations were at the Upper Manitou Lakes where mines with names like the Bigmaster, the Paymaster, the Little Master, the Laurentian, and the Detola appeared.

RESOURCEFULNESS

A strange looking former grocery is built around the headframe of a defunct mine. The reason? The owners realized that the cool air from the depths for the abandoned mine was ideal for keeping their produce cool.

Close by was the boom town of Gold Rock. Here was where the supplies came in, where the miners sent their children to school, where they worshipped and where some were buried. Here also was where the young, single miners would spend their pay on whiskey and painted ladies. It wasn't an easy place to get to. Travellers needed to disembark from the CPR trains at Wabigoon and cross Wabigoon Lake and then endure a jolting seven-kilometre journey along a wagon road to the site.

For one frenzied decade the Gold Rock mines were the focus of northern Ontario. Then, beginning around 1910, the deposits began to thin and the mines closed. The place was so remote from other centres that everyone left, and Gold Rock and its camps became ghost towns. A flurry of activity in the '30s failed to resuscitate the ghosts. In the 1970s, Ontario government researchers recommended preserving the ruins as a heritage site. But, typically, the proposals fell on deaf ears and the old shells continue to collapse.

GHOSTS OF THE SHUNIAH WEACHU

It is said that when legendary Ojibwa chief, Nanabijou, revealed to the Europeans the sacred site of the Shuniah Weachu, the native silver locations, the god Manitou turned him to stone, and he became the "Sleeping Giant" rock formation. The blame, however, more likely belongs with Chief Tchiatang of the Nipigon band for telling his son-in-law, prospector Oliver Daunais where it was.

The silver seekers knew there was silver in the area. They had found plenty of evidence along the shore of Lake Superior between Thunder Bay and the Sleeping Giant himself. In fact, the Prince's Mine was producing as early as 1846. In 1867, the Shuniah mine began bringing out silver at an incredible 2,000 ounces per ton. The Silver Harbour Mine operated between 1870 and 1877. Deposits were shallow and the mines short-lived.

But the great riches of the Shuniah Weachu lay west of Thunder Bay in a series of soaring rock mesas. To reach them the government built the Silver Mountain Highway. As Daunais and the others plodded along, chipping away at the rock outcrops, they made one silver discovery after another, and soon more than a half dozen mines were wrenching the silver from deep in the ground.

The Beaver

One of a cluster of mines, the Beaver, along with the Badger, the Porcupine, and the Rabbit, got off to a promising enough start. By 1887 its concentrator had produced nearly $100,000 in silver in a mere two months. The veins, however, were unpredictable; here rich, and there thin. Although the mines were finished by 1910, their yield was a respectable million dollars in silver.

Silver Mountain

On a high, windswept plateau lay the true Shunaih Weachu. The vein stretched for a mile across the summit and spawned two mining towns: Silver Mountain East End and Silver Mountain West End. At each site were sizeable villages with about three dozen log houses where census takers put the combined population at over 600. Their stamp mills were banging out 40 tons of ore a day, and by the turn of the century had produced more than a half million dollars in silver. The busy communities were put onto the list of "must-sees" for an 1899 tour for Ontario parliamentarians. Had they arrived just six years later, they would have been greeted with silence, for by then the silver deposits had been depleted and the mines shut. In 1906 the census takers could find no more than 60 people.

The Silver Mountain Highway is today a scenic back road that winds past the high rock mesas. However, the mines are overgrown, and only rubble remains. The ghosts of the Shuniah Weachu can rest in peace.

Cobalt Silver

Was it really true, as legend says, that when blacksmith Fred Larose threw his pick at a fox he discovered the deposit of silver that would turn a silent lake shore into a silver metropolis? It's more likely that the credit lies with a couple of timber scouts named McKinley and Darraugh. In 1902 the two were checking the forests around Long Lake for timber that would be suitable for railway ties. These were the years when the Ontario government was proposing a railway to open up the unusually rich farmlands that stretched northwest of Lake Timiskaming.

While resting on the shore of the small lake, they noticed a greyish rock that was unusually heavy. It was silver. Within a few short years the rocky shoreline had become an impossible tumble of shacks and a tangle of muddy roads. Those shacks became rambling wooden houses, and the roads became a main street with a half mile of stores. Cobalt had become a name known around the world, and a city of 10,000 by 1910. In addition to the boom-town stores were grander buildings, the exchange, the bank, and the Dutch style railway station revered for its arching two-storey waiting room.

Sadly for many of that 10,000, Cobalt was dry. To quench their thirsts, however, they had only to seek the nearest "blind pig", a bar disguised as a legitimate business, where they could buy their whiskey

153

and their women. No wonder that the newly formed Ontario Provincial Police quickly moved in and opened up a lockup.

> The mining museum and local service clubs have designed a drive-it-yourself tour to many of the abandoned mines that ring the town. Here the explorer can see old adits and gaze at the site of the legendary silver sidewalk. Beyond the signed route, the twisting roads lead to several other silent mines.

When they weren't boozing, the miners were hard at work in one of the 31 mines that dug into the hard rocks. So vast was the field that several of those mines had shafts beneath the very streets of Cobalt itself. Among them was the mine of the blacksmith, Fred Larose.

Cobalt prospered until the 1930s when the depression and plummeting silver prices killed all but one of the mines. The price plunged from more than $1.30 a ounce in 1920 to less than 28 cents in 1932. By the mid '30s, Cobalt's population stood at a mere 1,000.

Cobalt has since been ravaged by many fires. So much so that little of its remarkable heritage has survived. Gone now are the half mile of stores, and many of the miners' rambling wooden homes. Fortunately, the exchange, hotel, the bank and the railway station are still around.

Silver Centre

The success of the Cobalt silver fields sent the prospectors searching further for more silvery riches. Some of them headed up the Montreal River to Gowganda, others made their way down Lake Timiskaming to investigate rumours that somewhere down there lay another rich vein of silver. And they were not disappointed.

For a time it looked as though Silver Centre, 30 km south of North Cobalt, would rival Cobalt as queen of the silver fields. Along its narrow, twisting roads, and in its small cabins lived a community of 700. Cobalt was their link to with a branch of the railway that followed the Montreal River and the place boomed thanks to mines like Wettlaufer, Keeley and Frontier. It contained stores, a hotel, and a hockey team. But when it fell, it fell all the way. By the 1930s, only one or two of the mines were producing in spurts and that didn't last long either.

Although today Highway 567 from North Cobalt to the Montreal River Dam remains well travelled, not a soul lives in Silver Centre.

The small, wooden buildings have left scant remains. The only evidence that there was anything here at all are the tailings, a few shells of mine buildings, and here and there some rubble. These are the ghosts of Silver Centre.

Casey Cobalt

15 miles north of Cobalt, farmer David Bucknell thought that rocks in his back forty looked a lot like the ones he saw on his visits to Cobalt. And he was right, it was more silver. Although the vein was rich it was not extensive. Only one mine operated here, and its workforce was small. But by the time it had finished producing, the veins had given up nearly three million ounces of silver.

Silver Islet

Ontario's strangest ghost town story is that told by Silver Islet. It was strange in where it lay, and how it came to an end.

The 1840s were a time of frenzied searches for copper along the shores of Lake Superior; copper that natives had used to fashion trading goods. While looking for copper, James Woods landed on a tiny shoal off the tip of the Sibley Peninsula named Skull Rock. But with no way to mine the bounty, or to ship it, the waves continued to wash over it.

Once home to 700 people, Silver Centre has vanished almost completely.

155

In 1870, William Frue of Houghton, Michigan, just across the lake, convinced Major A.H. Sibley to buy the claim. In 1870 the miners started to arrive, and by 1872 Sibley had spent over one million dollars trying to bring the mine into production. Much of that was spent just on breakwaters. By the fall of 1870 a large breakwater had been put in place. However, the fall storms tossed it aside like a child's toy. Frue replaced it with a much larger breakwater. On March 18, a vicious storm during break-up hurled ice across the shoal washing everything into the lake,. Finally Frue completed a breakwater that was 75 feet wide at the base, 5 bulkheads deep, and stood over 18 feet high. In its bowels were 50,000 tons of rock. The breakwater held and Sibley began to recover his outlay, far more than even he could have anticipated.

On the tiny islet were the mine buildings and the bunkhouses. With miners of four different backgrounds, four bunkhouses were erected to keep them apart. On the mainland stood the town and the mill. More than 40 solid two-storey houses lined the shore. Here, too, were the Methodist and Santa Rosa Catholic Church, the company store, customs house, bank and jail. At the east end of "The Avenue"

A group of Miners rests in front of the shaft house on Silver Islet. Recreation was limited. Even though Silver Islet was legally supposed to be dry, Major Sibley turned a blind eye to miners' drinking as long as they obeyed his rules. Limiting them to three drinks a day, Sibley placed in the bar a blackboard with 300 squares on it: in each was a miner's payroll number. With every drink, the bartender would add a mark to keep count. Sibley ordered the bar to be 5 feet high so that none could jump it, at least not without some difficulty, and the fine for drunkenness was five dollars, or 10% of the miner's monthly pay.

The buildings on Silver Islet sat gaunt and empty once the waters of the lake flooded the shafts. Those same waters eventually took the buildings too.

were the half dozen larger houses of the managers, the grandest of all was the three-storey, wooden summer mansion of Sibley himself.

The mine had made Sibley fabulously wealthy. By 1883 it had brought from under the lake more than $3 million worth of silver. It was Canada's richest silver mine. But the veins were starting to thin out and in 1883 only $2000 in silver came out. To keep the shafts dry, furnaces were needed to pump the water out day and night. Even more vital was the winter coal supply. Without it the furnaces would turn cold and the shafts would flood. That winter the town's worst fears came true. The captain of the coal boat, H.B. Tuttle, found himself frozen in, rock solid. The coal supply never came. On the 1st of March the mine closed, and soon afterwards the miners moved away.

At the end of Highway 587, the miners' homes, the jail and the company store still stand. After the mine closed, the houses were bought up by residents of Port Arthur and Fort William to use as summer camps. Ghosts are plentiful. The little cemetery lies overgrown by the forest. A few of the buildings lie vacant, and the permanent population is a mere three. And the waves wash once more over the little shoal that once was Canada's richest silver mine.

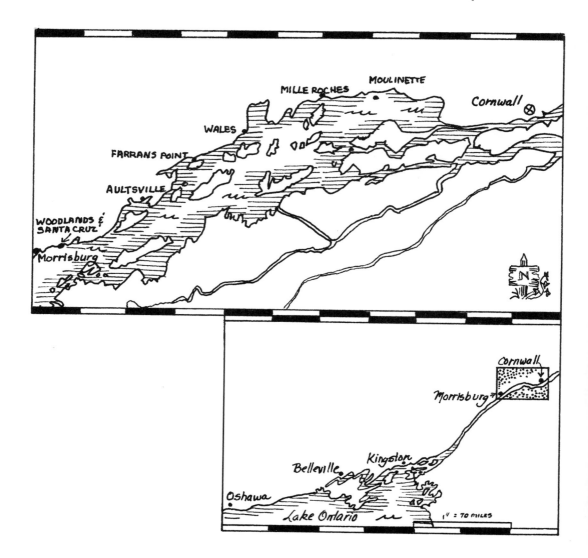

10

The Drowned Villages

~~~

Car wheels crackled on the gravel and stopped; headlights flicked silently off. Footsteps swished through the brown grass as thermoses, food-baskets and cases of beer plopped softly onto the ground. Arms wrestled with gangly wooden lawn chairs and bodies eased into the canvas webbing and waited. In the eastern sky the sun began to turn the grey, pre-dawn sky orange.

It was July 1, 1958, and thousands of spectators were flocking to the shores of the strangely dry St. Lawrence River to watch history. For this muggy summer morning marked the opening of one of the greatest construction projects ever accomplished — the St. Lawrence Seaway. As the sun inched higher, people checked their watches with more frequent anticipation. Finally, as the hands on the watches crept to 8:00, in the distance a muffled "whump" filled the air. It was the 30 tons of dynamite that tore open the coffer dams that for four years had held the river at bay. Rather than the roaring wall of water that some had expected, the inundation began as a trickle. Slowly and steadily it flowed around, then over the foundations, the roads, the backyards and the bridges of what had once been a string of pretty riverside villages. Four days later a new lake spread to the distant shore. Beneath it lay the drowned villages.

When the planners for the seaway began their drawings years earlier, they realized that at least one part of their job would be painful. They would have to tell 6,500 people in more than a half dozen villages that their homes and their very communities would be flooded and that they must move. For the planners it was at worst awkward; for the residents it was heartbreaking. The homes in which they had lived (some families for generations), the village shops in which they worked, the churches where they worshipped and their favourite fishing holes, all would be gone. And while many took pictures that

July morning, others shed a tear for those parts of their lives that would lie forever under the water.

The villages with names like Aultsville, Farrans Point, Wales, Mille Roches and Moulinette were among Ontario's earliest, some dating from the days of the French fur trade. Then the St. Lawrence was the earliest highway into the great lakes. Here the communities had grown up as important steamer stops or early lock stations on the St. Lawrence canals, which were built to bypass the mighty river's turbulent rapids. Mills, hotels and stores all flourished in these busy places.

Although the Seaway benefits primarily American Great Lake ports, the initiative to complete the linkage has always been Canada's. The first canals to bypass the rapids on the St. Lawrence were constructed in Canada in 1783, and by 1900 shallow canals finally connected Lake Superior with Montreal via the Welland Canal — again a Canadian project. It took a threat by the Canadian government in 1951 to build the new Seaway entirely on Canadian soil before the U.S. would participate. Even at that the Americans contributed only a third of what Canada did ($130 million compared to $330 million) toward the costs of construction.

The 20th century brought with it the changes that small villages all across Ontario experienced, and led to the demise of many of their businesses. None, however, became ghost towns; none until the 1950s when the massive new seaway was begun. More than 530 houses, stores, and churches were moved off their foundations and hauled to "new" towns with names like Long Sault and Ingleside. The remainder were simply levelled. The village of Iroquois was moved, almost in its entirety, a short distance back, while about a third of the village of Morrisburg was removed. Many of the most historic structures were hauled to one site, and from them a park was created. That park would grow into one of Ontario's premier tourist attractions — its name, Upper Canada Village.

But in their death the villages have attracted more attention than when they flourished. Today a "Lost Villages Society" preserves their memory, while guides like Ian Bowering's "Lost Villages Adventure", lead visitors along the new shorelines to gaze over the waters where the villages once stood, and divers from across North America search for the ruins of the early canals, and foundations of the old villages.

Mille Roches

The closest to Cornwall and to the huge dam that holds back the waters, Mille Roches lies the deepest below water. Deriving its name from the "thousands of rocks" taken from the early French limestone quarry, its 1200 residents made it the second largest of the drowned villages. They worshipped in one of three churches, sent their kids to the local public school, and played hockey in the arena. These sites now lie in up to 40 metes of water and are a half kilometre from shore. Here in the murky depths, divers have located the gates, the turbines and the other buildings of the earlier canals and power houses.

Moulinette

Whether it was named after the French word "moulin" for "mill", or "mounlinet" for the winches that the early voyageurs used will remain a mystery. Its ruins, however, will not, for these too are a popular destination for divers. Here, despite the high levels of silt, they seek out the wrecks and structures of the old canal. Settled by United Empire Loyalists the place also had five mills, two churches, a store and hotel, and in its later years, three tourist homes and a motel. Lakeview Park, on the relocated Highway 2, is the closest dry spot to the old village site.

Dickinsons Landing

Strategically located at the head of the boiling Long Sault Rapids, the site began as a landing for steamers. Around the wharf were a tannery, distillery and soap factory, while along its dusty streets were churches, six taverns, general stores and nearly 20 shops. By the time of the Seaway it had lost most of its shops and all of its industries and settled into being a quiet, riverside residential community. Today, it is the most popular of the drowned villages for divers. Here, in less than 20 metres of water, they find many relics from the old canal which had once guided ships past the town. Its lighthouse fared better and is now at Upper Canada Village.

Wales

A short distance inland, Wales developed as the Grand Trunk station grounds for Dickinson Landing. It took on its new name in 1860 when the Prince of Wales (later King Edward VII) stepped from the royal coach and walked along a bed of maple leaves to the landing to shoot the rapids in a steamer. A popular but frightening adventure for tourists, it was the 19th century version of white water rafting. The community was one of the smaller of the drowned villages, numbering 200 residents at its demise. A typical station village, it had stores, taverns, churches, and a number of houses. Most of these were moved to Ingleside. Unlike other sites, some of Wales remains above water, particularly Wales Island, where the foundations of St. Davids Anglican Church can be seen. It is located just offshore from the cemetery that sits on Highway 2 between Ingleside and Long Sault.

Farrans Point

Named after early settlers, Farrans Point had in its heyday four general stores, three blacksmiths and a pair of taverns, one of which remained a popular watering hole until the early 1950s. By the time of the Seaway it had only a pair of churches and stores. Today it is one of the more visible of the drowned villages. Being near the westernmost end of the flooded portion, it lies beneath only shallow waters, and in the fall and winter, some of the old sidewalks can be followed. It lies at Farran Point Park.

Aultsville

Like Farran's Point, parts of Aultsville remain above the flood line. Originally named Charlesville, it grew to include a small number of stores and shops. Its most important early industry was its brickyard and pottery, which supplied dishes and teapots for many of the area

Upper Canada Village. Created in 1955 by the Ontario government to preserve the historic buildings from the drowned villages. Located near Morrisburg, this living museum includes a farm, store, school, sawmill, cheese factory and woollen mill. A horse drawn boat recreates the technology used on the original St. Lawrence River canals.

The Aultsville Grand Trunk Railway station was rescued and moved a short distance from Upper Canada Village. Most of Aultsville's other buildings weren't so lucky.

pioneers. The waters covering its factory dump are shallow, making the area a popular destination for divers.

Aultsville, with its tree-lined streets and solid brick homes, was considered the prettiest of the lost villages. Sadly, few of its substantial structures could be moved and were subsequently demolished. One fortunate exception, the Garlough house, found its way to Upper Canada Village where park historians renamed it "Cooks Tavern". The Grand Trunk Railway Station was relocated to a park immediately west of Upper Canada Village. The old Aultsville Road now ends in a swampy bird sanctuary where old sidewalks and yards can be traced.

Woodlands and Santa Cruz

While these two places never amounted to "villages", Ian Bowering includes them in his "Lost Villages Adventure". Likely the site of pioneer landings or stopping places, the county atlas produced in the 19th century show both as being little more than a concentration of buildings. Prior to the flooding they were quiet residential communities with a few tourist facilities. Now, like the other villages of the drowned, they are covered forever by the waters of the mighty Seaway.

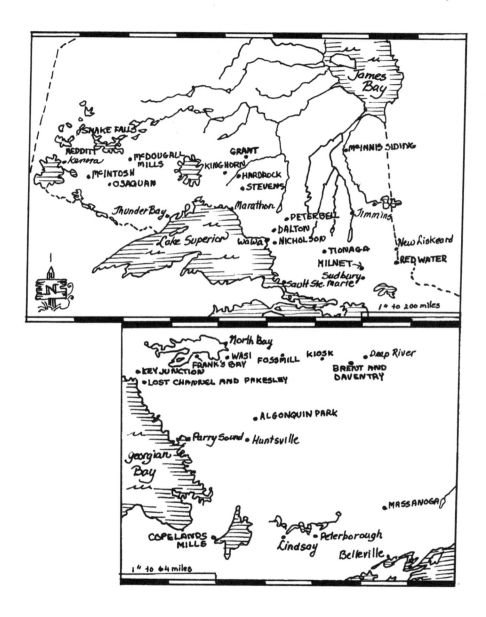

11

Steel Rail Blues:
The Railside Ghosts of the North
—⟨⟨⟩⟩—

While southern Ontario hummed with railways and factories, the north remained the land of canoes and fur posts. Although a few sawmill and mining towns hugged the shores of the larger lakes, it took the railways to bring industry to these hills and forests. While the results of this industrial onslaught are not universally hailed, the railways changed the face of the North irreversibly. From the earliest ground-breaking for the CPR in 1875 in West Fort William, to the driving of the Timiskaming and Northern Ontario Railway's (TNO) last spike 55 years later in Moosonee, the railways created new towns and whistlestops alike. The railways needed whistle-stops for no other reason than simply to make the trains run. Stations appeared at 8 to 12 mile intervals for the issuing of train orders and to supply coal and water. Every hundred miles or so were the divisional points. These were the all-important railway towns where train crews ended their runs, where engines were stored and maintained, and where trains were made up. While the smallest whistle-stops might contain simply the station and a few track workers' shacks, the divisional towns offered houses, hotels, stores, and often attracted other industries as well.

The railways opened up vast forests that until then had remained tantalizingly beyond the reach of the lumber companies. Soon the railways were lined with busy sawmill towns where the pungent smell of sawdust pierced the cold northern air, and smoke from the burners filled the skies. Part and parcel of many sawmill towns were the Hudson Bay fur posts. Once the railways brought with them a faster way of shipping pelts of mink, muskrat and beaver, the HBC gave up their water routes and moved to railside.

But as in the South, the face of the North began to change again. In the early 1950s, the Ontario government began turning over the North's forests to the huge multinational pulp companies and the sawmills were forced to

Horses strained to haul wagons piled high with logs from the northern forests.

close. During this period the railways began to change their fuel from coal to diesel and the whistlestops lost one of their key functions. When train movements began to be controlled electrically, they lost another. Because diesels were faster than the old coal burners, and needed fewer stops, many of the divisional towns closed their rail shops. The final straw, however, was the massive highway-building program of the 1950s and '60s. Funded partly by the federal government's "Roads to Resources" program, the subsidized road-building made the railways less economical. Passengers, no longer tied to the rail lines, took to their cars, and trucks took over the freight. Within a couple of decades the railside communities had become more of Ontario's vanished villages.

Lost Channel

For years lumber companies had been floating their logs from the forests of Parry Sound to their distant lumber mills. After MacKenzie and Mann had extended their Canadian Northern Railway north from Parry Sound in 1905, the Lauder Spear and Howland Lumber Company built a mill and company town on the shores of the narrow bay of Kawigamog Lake. Lost Channel contained a store, school, hospital, bunkhouse and houses for the workers. For a time the lumber was hauled by horses over a jolting logging road to the CNo at Mowat. Then in 1924 the Schroeder Company, which had by then taken over the mill, replaced the road with the Key Valley Railway, a short-line rail link to the CPR's new station at Pakesley. But the timber in the limits was getting scarce and in 1933, when the mill burned, they didn't bother to replace it. Today, a cottage road follows the old Key Valley roadbed from Highway 522 to a lodge which has moved into the old bunkhouse. Of the rest of the town and the landing, only rotting lumber and collapsed shells remain.

Pakesley

After the CPR built their Sudbury Junction branch linking Bolton and Sudbury in 1906, Pakesley began modestly enough. For the first few years of its life it was a typical whistle- stop with coal dock, water tank, a station and bunkhouses for the railway crews. That all changed when the Key Valley Railway was opened between Pakesley and the Schroeder Mill at Lost Channel. While a pair of steam engines handled the logs, a Model T Ford with flanged wheels shuttled passengers and light freight back and forth. Suddenly trains were puffing-in only a few minutes apart, depositing their load somewhere on the seven miles of siding the company had here. The CPR replaced the old station with one of its new, western-style stations with agent's sleeping quarters on the second floor, and a kitchen and dining room downstairs behind the ticket office. There was soon a hotel and a restaurant named Middy's. The Ontario Department of Lands and Forests brought their forestry station to the site, and Pakesley at its peak could count more than 30 buildings on either side of the sidings. Despite the demise of the Lost Channel Mill in 1933, Pakesley struggled on until the 1950s, when the store and post office closed. The station was demolished in 1971. Today, a half dozen vacant houses lurk in the bush near the Trans Canada Highway 69 at its junction with Provincial Highway 522.

Key Junction

Not far north of Mowat, the Canadian Northern Railway extended a spur line seven miles to Georgian Bay at Key Harbour. They used the harbour to import coal and export iron ore from the Moose Mountain Mine north of Sudbury. Their two-storey station was the largest building in the community. The junction also contained a general store and post office operated by John and Josephine Krystia, a railway bunkhouse, a school and four private houses. It remained a busy spot until 1955, when the railway closed the spur line in favour of using the harbour facilities at Depot Harbour. The station burned soon after, and in 1960 the tracks were lifted. Passengers riding VIA Rails "Canadian" through the old junction will still see the clearing, as well as a few sidings and a couple of old cabins, now used as hunting camps.

167

The Key Valley Railway hauled logs from Lost Channel to Pakesley. Both are now vanished villages.

Frank's Bay

Not all sawmill towns sat on the railway line. In 1885 the J.E. Smith Lumber Company opened a sawmill on an inlet on the south shore of Lake Nipissing called Frank's Bay. The railway, however, passed along the north shore and in the summer the village depended upon steamers such as the Laddie, the Seagull, and the Northern Belle, to link their isolated community with Sturgeon Falls and the CPR. In the winter, horses hauled the lumber across the ice. In 1888 the company opened a larger plant in Callander, on the new Northern and Pacific Junction Railway, and in 1905 closed the Frank's Bay Mill in favour of their railside location. A few cottages now stand where the old mill village once thrived.

Wasi

Frank's Bay was not the only lumber village on Lake Nipissing's south shore. Where the Wasi River flows into the lake, lumber baron J.R. Booth set up a log loading village. A short railway line linked the docks with his timber limits around Lake Nosbonsing. But when the Grand Trunk Railway finished their line into Callander, the Booth facility closed down. Today newer homes have taken over the site of this vanished mill village.

Algonquin Park

Most people travel to Ontario's magnificent Algonquin Park to seek tranquillity in wilderness. Strangely, the Park's wilderness is largely myth. Although established as a "national" park in 1893, it was in fact little more than a timber preserve for the lumber companies. One of the first mills to be built were those of the Gilmour Lumber Company at Mowat on the northwest shores of Canoe Lake. With a mill on the banks of Potter Creek, which flows into the lake here, the village dominated the western shore. At one point Mowat was said to have been home to 700 people. In 1898, however, the company was bankrupt, and most of the buildings were sold for scrap. A few survived and the old boarding house became the popular Mowat Lodge. Group of Seven artist, Tom Thomson, visited frequently and painted many scenes in Algonquin Park. It was while he was here that he drowned when his canoe upset in 1917. A few of the other Mowat houses are still used as cottages. However, when their leases expire near the end of the century, Ministry of Natural Resources will likely move in and remove this last bit of history.

In 1896 lumber baron J.R. Booth built his railway through the park. Along it were many little sawmill communities. A station village on the Booth line, Rock Lake became the site of the operations of the McCrea Lumber Company. A water tank, small station and few houses constituted the little railway, while the large sawmill of the lumber company stood nearby. It outlasted the railway by several years, finally closing its last mill in 1978. The railway bridge to the mill site is all that remains to indicate that any industry was ever here. The site is now the Rock Lake Campground.

Brule Lake, west of Canoe Lake, was another of the railside mill towns. Besides Duff's Mill the community contained a boarding house, school and a few cabins, as well as a small station. By the 1950s the mill had ceased operation and the Department of Lands and Forests removed the buildings. Rain Lake was the third little lumber town that stood on the Booth Line. Its location was west of Brule Lake near the Park's western boundary. It is accessible only by canoe, although like the others, all evidence of its existence has been removed.

For the most part, facilities for railway crew were spartan, such as this original restaurant in Brent.

Brent

Trains still rumble through the old communities of Brent and Daventry. They lie along the still active CN line that angles through the northern portion of the park. Brent was not just a mill town but a CN divisional town as well. The mill was operated by the Brent Lumber Company as recently as 1921, a few years after the line went through. The rest of the community consisted of small railway houses, a bunkhouse and a station. Although the Ministry of Natural Resources (MNR) stopped year round maintenance of the 50 kilometre dirt road into the site in the 1970s (despite the cries of protest by those who wished to live here), the place is still a busy cottage community, with many of the railway homes now summer cottages.

Daventry

A short distance west stand the remains of a section village called Daventry. Here stood a station, bunkhouse, cabins, and a one-room school covered in insulbrick. Although a few of these buildings still see seasonal use, access to the site is restricted.

Fossmill

In 1912 the Canadian Northern Railway hacked through Algonquin

Park a line linking North Bay and Ottawa. On the western end of the park, in reality little more than a timber reserve, William Foster started up a sawmill, and built beside it a townsite called Foster's Mills. In 1924, lumber baron S.J. Staniforth, needing a mill to cut the timber from his newly acquired Algonquin pine limits, bought Foster's mill and changed the name of the townsite to Fossmill. From the mill he built a railway spur line to Tee Lake, and along it operated two locomotives that could haul 15 loads of logs every day. The population grew to about 175 men plus their families. Enrolment in the school alone stood at 50. The division of the town almost mirrored Canada's historic two solitudes. While the workers were largely French and Catholic and lived on one side of the tracks, management was English and Protestant and lived on the other. They lived and worked together until 1934 when the mill, like so many, burned. Fossmill declined until the 1950s when only six families remained. Today the site, which lies east of Powassan on Highway 11, leaves no trace other than a few dirt trails which were the roads, and some cellar holes which were the houses that lined them.

Kiosk

Despite being burned out at Fossmill, Staniforth had bigger things in mind; the late J.R. Booth's vast timber limits, also in the park. In 1938 he built a new mill on the same railway just a few miles east, at the site of Booth's old bunkhouse on Kioshkakwia Lake. Here he developed a company town of 75 houses and a population of nearly 300. Kiosk added a school and large Roman Catholic church and prided itself on its hockey team. But few sawmills escape the inevitable flames, and in 1973 Staniforth's Kiosk suffered that fate as well. Following the fire, the Ministry of Natural Resources invoked a new policy that Algonquin Park perhaps should be something of a wilderness after all and refused to let Staniforth rebuild. Then they went further. They turned to the townspeople and ordered them out too. Not inclined to be forced from the place they called home, they rallied their MP and MPP to their cause and talked the MNR into a compromise. No longer ordering them out, the Ministry advised them that while they may leave whenever they wished, they would nonetheless have to sell their homes to the government, so that they

171

might demolish them. In 1980 most of the town still stood. However, a mere decade later only three buildings remained. The MNR had removed all: the church, the school and the 75 houses. And, myopically, they even demolished one of their own buildings, the century-old Booth bunkhouse.

South of Highway 17, between North Bay and Mattawa, Kiosk remains popular with canoers as a starting point for trips through northern Algonquin Park. While there may be a little more wilderness here now, there is a lot less history.

Milnet

Located 12 km north of Capreol, Milnet was another railside mill town. In 1917, a few years after the Canadian Northern Railway had built through the area, the Marshay Lumber Company established a mill and townsite on the shores of Onaping Lake. Two dozen look-alike company houses lined the neat streets opposite the two-storey railway station. By the time the Second World War exploded, the timber was gone and the company closed its operation. Most of the houses were burned or removed. Several foundations and at least a couple of the old homes still stand. The station, alas, has gone. In its place stands the usual tin shed for maintenance crews.

Tionaga

The disenfranchisement and internment of Japanese Canadians during World War II was one of the worst atrocities committed by our nation in recent history. Uprooted and deprived of the property they had worked hard to acquire, many were shipped like prisoners to British Columbia's interior ghost towns to wait out the war years. In Ontario, the abandoned sawmill town of Tionaga, on the tracks of the CNR west of Timmins, played the same, distasteful role.

Tionaga, with its large two-storey station, was a sawmill town operated by the Acme, then the Pineland Lumber Company. It had the usual assortment of cabins and bunkhouses along with a post office and a population of 150. But the North's railside lumbermen had to be prepared to move to where the fresh stands of timber waited. In 1937, Pineland moved the mill to Shawmere, and Tionaga sat empty. Three years later the cabins were still solid, and trains from

This historic lumber camp was levelled to make way for a fish camp.

the west coast began unloading their prisoners, many of them ill-prepared for the biting northern winters. When the war ended, most of the Japanese Canadians returned to the West Coast, while a few remained to pursue careers in the logging industry in Northern Ontario.

When Pineland returned to the area to open a camp on nearby Horwood Lake in 1953, they used Kukatush as their station, and CN moved the Tionaga station to that site. The cabins remained at Tionaga, empty and deteriorating. Many were burned by vandals. Others were removed or just collapsed. Today only scattered lumber tells of the high points and the low points of this remote whistle-stop.

Meanwhile, down at Horwood Lake, Pineland closed its operation (in 1957) and moved once more to Timmins. On the shores of the lake the bunkhouses, cookery and sawdust burner stood for nearly twenty years — a rare and photogenic ruin — until they were removed to be replaced by a fishing camp.

Peterbell

Peterbell was a sawmill town on the CNR west of Foleyet. The town contained single houses, two rows of bunkhouses for mill workers and facilities for railway workers as well. The commissary contained a

173

pool table, juke box and hosted dances and movies. There was a one-room school, but the utter isolation proved too much for most teachers, and few lasted more than a year. The Hudson's Bay Company relocated its store here in 1925, while the Lacroix' operated a private boarding house. The timber was trucked from one of several logging camps which ringed Missinaibi Lake. While life in Peterbell was relatively sedate, that in the camps was considerably more boisterous, fuelled often by the copious consumption of bootleg booze. The first company in the area was the Missinaibi Lumber Company which operated until the 1950s when it was replaced by the Pineland Lumber Company. The mill was steam-operated and lasted until 1963. Since then all buildings have been removed and the once busy mill town is now just a clearing in the forest that flashes by the train windows, unnoticed and largely forgotten.

Biscotasing

That much of this partial ghost town still stands is a tribute to the heritage enthusiasm of the handful of residents who linger here. In the 1880s it was a rowdy rail's end for CPR construction crews. But they eventually moved on to make Chapleau the divisional point, and "Bisco" settled down to become a sawmill town. The rocky hillsides that overlooked Biscotasi Lake became covered with solid two-storey

As with this HBC post in Biscotasing, many fur trading operations moved railside with the arrival of the railways. This one burned.

174

homes, presided over by the Catholic church which claimed the highest point of land. By the station were the general store and the Hudson's Bay Post, while the Booth and Shannon Mill sprawled over a point of land in the lake. Biscotasing was briefly home to one of Canada's legendary characters, the wiley "Chief" Grey Owl. It was here that the "chief" lived a rollicking life as the real life Archie Belaney; too rollicking, for he fled town after a knife fight and joined a local native band where he decided to become "Grey Owl" and devote his life to preaching and writing on wildlife conservation. Meanwhile, the town got along without him just fine until the mill, typically, burned to the ground. After that, Bisco's population plunged from a high of nearly 300 to a mere dozen or so. More recent logging operations in nearby Ramsay have brought a few more residents into the town's old buildings and its population has crawled back over 50. The historic townsite still retains many old buildings, some empty, some reused and some used seasonally as camps. While the churches and several houses survive, the station and the original stores no longer stand.

Nicholson

So plentiful and picturesque were the ruins of this ghost town, that in 1975 the government of Ontario actually contemplated establishing a ghost town park. However, cooler anti-heritage heads within the Ministry of Natural Resources prevailed and the idea was scrapped. The town began with the tie mill built by James Austin and George Nicholson in 1910 and contained two churches, a 70-room hotel, and several one and two-storey houses. Although the town was "dry", workers needed only to board a train for the short 12 mile trip into Chapleau to the east, a town which, according to some, possessed ample forms of late evening entertainment. The mill burned in 1938 and Nicholson was abandoned. Many of the houses were later bought for use as cottages, a function which many still perform. By 1975, however, the former main street resembled one from wild west movies, and inspired a pair of imaginative government heritage planners to propose to their higher-ups the idea of a ghost town park. But the hierarchy wasn't interested and a few years later, when a hungry hunter used the wrong fuel to light his stove, that main street burned

175

Nicholson

above: Had the government accepted advice from its historians, the old Nicholson store might have survived. Instead, it burned.

right: Although much has been destroyed, Nicholson retains many photogenic ruins.

bottom: Highly maneuverable, the boats used to manipulate the log booms were called alligators. This one was used at Nicholson.

How to find Nicholson:
By VIA Rail westbound from Chapleau. By canoe from Shoals Provincial Park.

down. Nevertheless, there is still much to see here on the north shore of Windermere Lake: an old church whose steeple sags a little more every year, weathered cabins, home only to critters, and the two-storey school. The train still stops here to allow cottagers to disembark, but only three times a week now, and most explorers arrive by boat from the lake's south shore.

Dalton

In 1922, Austin and Nicholson added to their empire, building a sawmill several miles west of Nicholson at Dalton. By 1925 the site was one of the largest along the line, with a store, two churches, three dozen houses and a two-storey bunkhouse. There were two Daltons: the mills on the Shakwamkwa River, a few miles west of the railway, and, the townsite beside the tracks. In 1949 the river mill burned, for the second time and the townsite was cleared. Operations continued on and off at the track and continue to do so. By the river only rubble and a badly overgrown cemetery remain. More survives by the track. A few of the original company houses, a church, and old village streets that make their way past overgrown yards, give the place a decidedly ghostly appearance. Dirt trails lead both east to the track and west to the river from Highway 651 north of Highway 101 in the Missanaibi area.

Stevens

When other sawmill towns were closing down, Stevens was just getting started. In the years following the Second World War, the Ontario government was revoking the timber rights it had granted to small sawmill companies and turning them over to large, multinational pulp and paper companies, like Marathon. While that company was building a massive mill and creating a townsite around it that would become the town of Marathon, it also opened a number of camps in the forests. More than a hundred miles to the north, along the CNR, it opened Stevens. By the early 1950s, it had a school, hospital, curling rink, and three dozen houses, and census takers were able to count 460 residents. However, by the mid-1960s the main area of cutting had moved west, and Stevens was closed. Because it was a company town, everything was removed, and today this once busy place is little more than an overgrown clearing in the middle of a regenerating forest. It lies on a forest road between Manitouwadge and Caramat.

Kinghorn
Located west of Geraldton on the CNR, Kinghorn began as a section village for the railway. When the gold stampede struck the area in the 1930s, it became the jumping-off point for prospectors using Partridge Lake. In 1948 a sawmill was built and with the bunkhouses for the workers, the rough and tumble camp became a busy spot. But the mill survived only a decade. By 1960, with the gold rush long passed, the mill closed, and the railway facilities removed, Kinghorn fell vacant. Only a few collapsed and vandalized cabins litter the overgrown site.

Hardrock
Like Kinghorn, Hardrock Station became a jumping-off point for the Little Longlac gold rush. Because it was located on the shores of Long Lake, it was convenient for gold seekers to outfit themselves here before slipping their canoes into the cold waters to scour the shores for the telltale glitter of gold. A sizable settlement grew up at trackside, with a bank, hotel and Maude Gascon's restaurant. The station was only a single-storey building and when it needed enlarging, the CNR simply added a boxcar to the end of it. Confident that the place was on the verge of becoming a boom town, Mrs. Gascon laid out a town-site, and waited for the money to roll in. But she asked too much, and when the Geraldton townsite began growing soon after, her land proved worthless. But her woes didn't end there. In 1936 a horrific forest fire ravaged the area and the helpless Hardrock stood right in its path. The place never recovered from the devastation.

Osaquan
For a while in the 1920s, the mill town of Osaquan on the CPR west of Ignace, was the largest town between Ignace and Kenora. It began life in 1890, not unlike many railway towns, as a jumping off point for prosectors, these bound for the Sturgeon Lake gold fields. When the National Transcontinental Railway (NTR) opened to traffic further north in 1915, Savant Lake was closer for the prospectors, and

the landing at Osaquan fell silent. That's when D.L. Mather purchased the property and built a sawmill and a company town. In it were bunkhouses, cabins, a cookery and a school. In 1921 the population stood at nearly 150. In 1931 the mill burned and was rebuilt but with the timber largely depleted it failed to fully recover. By the time the Second World War erupted, the last of the buildings (the school) was demolished. Today all traces have vanished, save for a bit of rubble, and the activity here now is that of cottagers heading for their camps on Camp Lake.

McDougall Mills

When the NTR opened its line through Northwestern Ontario, it passed close to the Sturgeon River. The river's extensive network allowed the lumber company to establish a sawmill that took advantage of both the river and the track. While the store and bunkhouses lined the track, the mill stood on a point of land in the wide river. Between 1917 and 1954, it was the largest community between Sioux Lookout and Savant Lake. When the timber supply was depleted and a larger mill opened up in Sioux Lookout, with the all-important highway access, the sawmill on the river closed. While a few ruins remained until the 1970s there is little to see today.

McIntosh

The largest operation at McIntosh was the Catholic Indian Residential School. The school was started by one Father Gauthier in 1925 and grew to house 175 students. The building stood three stories high and the grounds contained kitchens, barns, playgrounds and dormitories. Most students arrived by train at the McIntosh station. The school burned in 1965, and the grounds have remained vacant since then. Only the church has survived. At McIntosh station, the fine old depot has gone, replaced by the usual tin shed.

Snake Falls

When the Red Lake gold rush was at its frenzied peak in the 1930s, the building boom required an almost inexhaustible supply of lumber. Where the Chukuni River tumbles into Pakwash Lake, the Chukuni Lumber Company built a sawmill and small company town. By the company store were a dozen or so workers' cabins and what was called a native shanty town. In the late 1940s, the new highway linking Red Lake with the CNR to the south opened, and the new town of Ear Falls became the heart of the area. In 1955 the lumber company moved its operation to Ear Falls and closed the mill at Snake Falls. Shortly afterwards a fire destroyed much of what remained. The site lies a short distance west of Highway 105 about halfway between Ear Falls and Red Lake.

Redditt

Without divisional points railways could not run. Here crews ended their runs and stayed overnight to return home. Roundhouses and engine houses provided maintenance and storage for steam engines while large railway stations contained offices for supervisors and dispatchers.

Redditt was a divisional point halfway between Sioux Lookout and Winnipeg, on the NTR, Wilfred Laurier's "national dream." The yards sprawled across the little valley with a solid two-storey station on the south side, and engine house and roundhouse on the north side. Houses, stores and other town buildings sat on the hillsides on each side of the valley. The town's grandest day occurred in 1939 when the gold and blue coaches of the royal train carrying King

The now quiet town of Redditt put on its Sunday best when the royal train puffed into the station in 1939.

George VI and Queen Elizabeth on their six week rail odyssey across Canada, pulled into the station for the scheduled 20 minute stop. Dressed in their finest clothes, the residents crowded the station for a glimpse of the royal couple. After a brief appearance, the pair returned to their coach and the train puffed off down the track.

By 1960 Redditt's grand days were done. By then diesel had replaced coal and trains were running longer and faster. Divisional points were no longer needed every 100 miles, and Redditt was closed down. Its population plunged from over 300 to less than 150. The tracks were lifted, the station was demolished and the roundhouse closed. A road was built to connect Redditt with Kenora and today those who remain commute. In place of the fine station, a string of nondescript aluminum sheds for maintenance workers line the track. Many of the town buildings are gone, and the roundhouse is now a repair shop. In place of the large yards where sidings full of boxcars once stood, there is now an airstrip.

Grant

When the NTR opened their line, their next divisional point east of Armstrong was Grant. It had the usual offices, yards, roundhouse and town buildings. Then in 1923 the Canadian National took over the bankrupt NTR, which had become part of the Grand Trunk, and the equally bankrupt Canadian Northern Railway as well. Where the two lines bent close to each other near Longlac, the CNR built a connection. Grant, however, was too far east to continue as a divisional point for the now connected lines. The CNR then selected a better location and hoisted Grant's buildings onto a string of flat cars and moved it to the new site. Nakina, the name given the new site, grew into a town of more than 1000 people with a main street lined with hotels and stores, and large railway homes on the several residential streets. Today, although that population has dwindled to about 700, it remains an active place. The divisional operation has closed down here as well. However, to honour their railway heritage the townspeople rescued their station from vandalism and deterioration, and have preserved it. Meanwhile, back down the line at Grant, even the tracks have been removed, and the forests have reclaimed the site.

181

McInnis Siding

As the Timiskaming and Northern Ontario Railway (TNO) extended their tracks northward from Cochrane in the 1920s, they opened up access to more timberlands. On the banks of the Abitibi River, the Hawk Lake Lumber Company built a sawmill, shingle mill, and created a small townsite. The remote little community could claim a store, office, bunkhouses, steam bath, and several houses for workers and their families. They fought the depressing isolation by holding dinners and dances in the recreation centre, or getting together with residents of the now dismantled Hydro settlement at Island Falls, a short distance north. But the blisteringly cold northern winters at times made them wonder if it was all worth it. By 1962 the operation was being run by the Wicks Company who in that year moved their operations to their facility in Timmins and closed that at McInnis Siding. While most useful material was carted away, there yet remain the crumbling remains of a few old structures. They are almost impossible to reach, hidden by forest, and ignored by the trains of the Ontario Northland Railway (ONR) that simply now speed past.

Redwater

By contrast a number of the buildings in Redwater still survive. Passengers riding the trains may wonder at the string of cabins that flash past the window, seemingly in the middle of nowhere. A former TNO section and mill village, Redwater was typical of many northern communities in that respect. "The middle of nowhere" was where the sawmills and the rail crews were needed. These settlements, which were too small to qualify for schoolhouses, were served by the rolling school cars, passenger coaches outfitted as classrooms and deposited on sidings for a week at a time so that the children, and sometimes the adults could get an education that was otherwise out of their reach. The enrolment in the school car at Redwater peaked at 16 in the early 1950s. When the mill was closed, it and the other company buildings were dismantled. While a station nameplate still stands by the track, only the former boarding house and a couple of cabins survive, some of them used by hunters. Access is by boat from the end of Rabbit Lake Road east of Highway 11, south of Cobalt.

Copeland Mills

While Simcoe County is far from Northern Ontario, the story of Copeland Mills shares many similarities with its northern cousins. In 1906 when the CPR opened its branch line to Sudbury, Jasper Martin acquired a large tract of forest in a lowland by the track and built a sawmill. While Martin operated the mill the place was called Martinville. Then in 1922 Charles Copeland bought the then idle mills and changed the name to Copeland Mills. He laid out a small company town with a store, school, and several cabins for workers and their families. The buildings had a decidedly "Cape Cod" appearance with their wood shingle sidings. Under Copeland the mills became the largest in the county, capable of turning out 10,000 board feet of lumber a day. Then in 1959 the large mill burned and was replaced with a smaller one. Fewer workers were needed and the number of houses dropped from seven to four. In 1960 rail shipment ended, and in 1975 the mill burned again. This time it was not replaced. Three years later the Copelands sold the property to the Ministry of Natural Resources. They maintained the company office and manager's house for a few years and then, typically, demolished them. Today the site of the little town is a parking lot for hunters.

Massanoga

Massanoga was another example of a "northern" style sawmill town in Southern Ontario. Although the 19th century lumber companies had pretty well cleared Southern Ontario of its forest, enough new timber stood in the 1930s to interest the Sawyer Stoll Lumber Company of Michigan in establishing a mill and company town in the middle of what would become cottage country. Near Mazinaw Lake, the site of the celebrated Bon Echo Rock, the town consisted of three bunkhouses, a recreation hall, a school and about a dozen houses. In 1945 the company moved its planing mill to the CPR trackside at Kaladar, and in 1962 shut down the Massanoga operations completely. Ten years later they refurbished the mill and briefly brought life back to the site, but that soon ended, and the buildings were removed. Today, by the shores of Stoll Lake west of Highway 41, cottagers and hunters taking the bush trail pass only a clearing and the shell of the mill.

12

All That Glistens Is Not Gold: Ontario's Industrial Minerals

O ver the history of Ontario, many minerals were yanked from the ground for their industrial value. Some such as iron and nickel are still valued for that purpose. Others have been replaced by different materials or superior technologies: corundum is no longer the world's hardest mineral, graphite has little commercial use, while mica and feldspar are minerals familiar to few except geologists and rock collectors. Yet all these minerals were searched out, mines built atop the deposits, and villages created nearby for the workers and their families. These unglamorous minerals were often worth their weight in gold, and have resulted in some of Ontario's more interesting and extensive vanished villages and ruins.

SUDBURY NICKEL

In 1889 a Scottish scientist named James Riley turned the mining world on its ear when he proclaimed the value of a mineral most had thought useless — nickel. He proved how hard and resistant nickel could be and promoted its value as an insulator and for its use in armour.

A remote rocky region of northern Ontario would prove to contain the world's greatest deposits. When an enormous meteor smashed into the earth millions of years ago, the tremendous heat mineralized rocks over a huge area. This area, the Sudbury Basin, contains vast amounts of minerals, the most valuable of which are copper and nickel. The prospectors who had scoured the hills around Sudbury for copper, had given nickel little thought. When discoveries of copper brought the Canada Copper Company into the area, they named their company town Copper Cliff, a name that it retains to this day. But with Riley's revelation, all eyes turned to nickel.

While mines appeared over an area 50 miles long and 10 miles wide, the focus of the area became the company town of Copper Cliff, with its planned streets, its hospital, school, recreation clubs, and houses. Smaller mines provided bunkhouses, and other facilities for the miners on site. Although Sudbury still produces nearly a quarter of the world's nickel, many of the smaller mines — nearly 30 in number — have closed, and most of the refining is done at Copper Cliff with its legendary "big stack", and at Falconbridge. But throughout the scarred hillsides, there still linger the tailings, the foundations, and the old village streets of Sudbury's ghost mines.

Victoria Mines

Of Sudbury's abandoned nickel mines, the Victoria was the largest. Discovered by prospector Henry Rodger in 1886, it was not until 1906 that the place boomed. In that year Ludwig Mond erected a smelter to test a new process. A townsite with 200 lots was laid out and soon acquired a restaurant, a barber, five stores and a station on the CPR. At its peak, Victoria Mines, about six kilometres west of Whitefish, could count a population of nearly 1,000. But in 1923, with the deposits in the 2,600 foot deep shaft thinning out, the mine

The smelter and station at Victoria Mine have gone, along with everything else, except for a solitary dwelling, tailings and a track in a meadow.

186

closed and the town vanished. While the networks of streets remain as gravel trails in a meadow, only a single house, and the tailings, survive to tell the story of this nickel ghost.

Worthington

The Worthington Mine went not with a whimper but with a bang. On October 3, 1927, a shift boss named Ballentyne entered the shaft far beneath the ground at the third level. As his eyes grew accustomed to the darkness, he began to notice movement in the wooden pillar that supported the main shaft. He felt a cold shiver run along his back. If he didn't act fast the entire mine would collapse killing all within it. He quickly rammed extra poles against the weakening rock and then worked against time to hurry the miners out. They passed an anxious night. Then at 5:50 in the morning, with a tremendous shudder, the mine collapsed. More than seven million tons of rock and clay crashed through the shafts. Before that it had been one of the area's earliest working mines (following the Murray Mine into production in 1894) and one of its richest. The community had several winding cinder streets with workers' homes along them, and claimed a station on the CPR. Today, while a highway sign still announces "Worthington" and a few new buildings now line Highway 658, the dirt streets wind through empty meadows, and the wind wafts the grasses where the houses and cabins once stood.

The Chicago

Many smaller mines operated briefly. On Highway 658 about seven kilometres north of Worthington, sat the Chicago Mine. It began operation in 1889 as the Travers Mine and could claim a smelter from which the ore was shipped to Youngwood, Ohio for refining. But its owner, the Drury Nickel Company, went bankrupt, and after a few years the mine closed.

The Gertrude

This, too, lies in a remote area of woodland about four kilometres west of where the town of Creighton once stood. Opened in 1892, and later bought by the Lake Superior Power Company, the Gertrude sent its ore to Sault Ste. Marie for refining. The company

The roasting pit at O'Donnell, although gone for decades, destroyed vegetation for miles around and the area has still not recovered.

later built a smelter on the site where ore from the nearby Elsie mine was refined as well. In 1918 the company collapsed and was purchased by the British American Nickel Company, which itself was soon out of business. The Gertrude and the Elsie have lain dormant since then.

O'Donnell

There is a dirty little environmental secret lurking in the remote rocks west of Sudbury. This was O'Donnell, the site of a deadly open air roasting pit. Ore was hauled here on flat cars and roasted on outdoor furnaces. Opened during the First World War, the roast yard consisted of four parallel tracks, each about 7,500 feet long, with the ore piled between. The wood beneath was set ablaze and the ore was left to roast for several months. The process removed the sulphur from the ore, making it easier to mill. However, while the ore roasted, deadly clouds of sulphur dioxide crept across the countryside, killing vegetation for miles around. Although the process was banned more than a half century ago, the landscape has never recovered. Located about seven kilometres northeast of the village of Whitefish, on an abandoned section of the former Algoma Eastern Railway, the foundations of the roasting pit and the remains of the sidings are still visible amid this barren landscape.

Nickelton

With the demand for nickel soaring during the First World War, the British American Nickel Company moved to acquire several nickel properties around Sudbury. The area's first mine, the Murray, was to become the site for the company's smelter. Employees would commute by rail from Sudbury, four miles away. But by the time the smelter began operation, the war was almost over. The company, which had existed strictly for the war effort, folded, and the smelter was abandoned. Although INCO owns the site today, ruins of the smelter still linger in the weeds and brush.

Creighton

The threat of environmental disaster, reminiscent of Buffalo's deadly Love Canal, devastated some communities just as surely as the depletion of the mineral deposit. The Creighton Mine was and still is one of INCO's most productive, and the townsite, built around the turn of the century, was one of the company's largest. At its peak, more than 1,200 residents enjoyed the 400 solid homes, the churches and the busy main street. Adjacent to the bustling city of Sudbury, its citizens couldn't ask for anything more. But what they got, they could never have expected. In 1986 Ontario's environment ministry advised INCO that the underground service that provided the homes with water and sewers were failing badly. To bring them up to standard would cost INCO $10.5 million and the company decided it no longer wanted to play landlord. They gathered together the anxious residents who heard their worst fears realized. Their town was about to die.

Within two years, the place had been evacuated, and every building removed, except the mine structures at the Number Nine Shaft, which, at more than 2,000 metres, was the world's deepest. Today sidewalks and foundations, overgrown gardens, and here and there rusting swing sets and tricycles, are sad reminders of this once happy and proud community.

Happy Valley

Like Love Canal, the name belies the fate of the community. Located in a shallow valley beside the solid company town and smelters of

Falconbridge, northeast of Sudbury, Happy Valley suffered the effects of temperature inversions. Under certain climatic conditions, the sulphurous fumes from the Falconbridge refinery would wrap the community in a deadly shroud. In 1965, health officials reacted, ordering everyone out. The government bought the buildings and demolished most. Today the little valley resembles a desert, burnt and lifeless, except for the rubble and silent streets of the little place that the residents once called "Happy Valley."

IRON IN THE GROUND

Although it never stirred men to dream of wealth the way gold did, iron was probably the most essential mineral in 19th century Ontario. While iron is usually associated with massive and smoky factories, Ontario's earliest iron producers looked for it in swamps. The first iron furnace was in the eastern Ontario town of Lyndhurst and began operation in 1800. But the poor quality of the ore doomed the operation to a short life span.

Normandale

One of those early producers was Joseph Van Norman. The area around Potter's Creek on the shores of Lake Erie contained large quantities of bog ore and it was here in 1820 that Van Norman bought up an earlier operation owned by John Mason. The area was also rich in maple, oak and beech, the perfect trees for making the all-important charcoal, an essential ingredient in processing the ore. The little valley was soon alive with Ontario's earliest iron industry. Van Norman laid out streets and the community grew to a population of 300. On those streets were, according to traveller William Smith in 1846, a blacksmith, a store, a tavern, a tailor and two shoemakers.

Van Norman's furnaces operated 10 months a year, producing four tons of iron a day. The iron went into producing the utensils needed by Ontario's early farmers: stoves, kettles and farm implements. Had Smith arrived a year later, he would have found the furnaces cold, the village empty. For by the then the ore supply was depleted, and Van Norman had blown out his furnace and moved on. As the village withered, the furnace lay buried until unearthed by archaeologists more than a century later. The hotel lasted that long as well, and today functions as a tea room. Most of the other buildings are gone, although many of the old village lots now claim newer homes.

Olinda

While he operated Van Norman had only one rival. That was the furnace of Cahoon and Field several miles west in Essex County. Here on Lot 21, Concession 5 of Gosfield Township, they blew in a furnace in 1834 and erected a stack 30 feet high. Using bog ore from the vicinity, the operation used up to 100 men. Their village was called, aptly, "The Furnace". By 1840 the operation had ceased and today the site is part of a farm.

Blairton

From Normandale, Van Norman headed to the then remote wilderness, north of Rice Lake. Here, at Marmora, the site of an ironworks since 1822, Charles Hayes had discovered in the hard rocks by the shores of Crowe Lake an iron deposit so massive and rich that he nicknamed it "the big ore bed". The problem lay in its remoteness. The lengthy shipping route — via road, Rice Lake then road again — put the market cost at $30 a ton. When the St. Lawrence canals were enlarged a few years later, imported iron cost only $16 a ton and the furnace at Marmora shut down. In 1867, when the Cobourg Peterborough and Marmora Railway opened and extended a spur line to the mine, the Marmora furnaces started up again.

By the deposit, a few miles west, the mining village of Blairton was laid out. Here on 11 streets were over 200 lots, 40 miners' cottages, two stores, two hotels, boarding houses, a church, a school and a population of 500.

But the problem of remoteness continued to plague the operation and in 1875 it closed once more. By 1900 only 25 people remained. Today the street pattern can still be traced, a couple of old cabins and foundations along them. The area is returning to life with recreational trailer grounds and other forms of rural sprawl.

Irondale

If Van Norman was Ontario's first iron king, Charles Pusey may have been its greatest. This Pittsburgh native arrived in Ontario sometime

191

around 1880 and began scouting the ground for signs of iron. By then the railways had penetrated Ontario's onetime wilds and remoteness was less of a problem. In 1881 he bought up the operations in Haliburton that had been started by Parry and Miles, and probed the ground a little deeper. Near the shores of Salerno Lake he uncovered an extensive deposit. Immediately he laid out a village and built a railway to the site; the precursor to the beloved Irondale, Bancroft and Ottawa Railway. Irondale was born. The town grew to contain two stores, three hotels and a church. Its population at one point stood at over 500, most of whom toiled by the two blast furnaces that turned out 20,000 tons of pig iron a year.

By 1900 the deposits were depleted, and the furnaces were blown out. The population slid to fewer than 30. The stores closed and one of the two hotels was dismantled and moved to Peterborough. The railway station burned in the 1930s, and today, on the village streets, only the old church survives.

Wilbur

Here too the building of a railway paved the way for new iron mines. In this case it was the Kingston and Pembroke Railway (which never reached Pembroke) and the Wilbur Mine. By 1888 the mine was in full swing, as was the town of Wilbur with a population counted at 200. Over its life the mine shipped nearly 125,000 tons of iron, most of it to Sault Ste Marie, before closing in 1911. Today the old K & P Railway is a bush road that leads south from the hamlet of Lavant Station (called "Iron City" when the mines were operating) to the old mine, where the tailings, an overgrown cemetery, and a pair of old houses are Wilbur's sole survivors.

Robertsville

From its first mine, the Lizzie, Robertsville (20 km south of Wilbur), grew into a sizeable company town. Near the spur line from the K&P Railway were 28 duplex houses, along with a store and boarding houses. The mine was renamed the Mississippi, after a nearby river, and went on to yield nearly 7,000 tons a year before closing in 1901. Today the once busy village has vanished and the site is covered with a new growth of trees. Only a cemetery on a distant hillside recalls the early days when iron ruled this little hollow. And, had the name of the village not survived in the name of the road, even the memory of the place would have vanished.

Glendower

The road sign on Highway 38 says "Godfrey". However it was here that a spur line branched west from the K&P to the Zanesville or Glendower mine. It did well, yielding 50,000 tons over its 20 year life. Today traces of the spur line are so vague as to be indiscernible, and all evidence of the mine has gone. At Godfrey, however, a large wooden general store that was built in a time when the mine promised greatness to the area, still stands.

Bessemer

While it was the gold that made central Hastings County famous, it was the countless iron deposits that prompted the building of the Central Ontario Railway. In 1900, a nine-mile spur line, named the Bessemer and Barry's Bay Railway, was built from the COR to the iron deposits at Bessemer (named after Henry Bessemer, who perfected the process for manufacturing steel from iron). Two mines operated at the site, the Bessemer and the Childs (or Rankin), shipping as much as 3,000 tons in their first year of operation, and 100,000 over

Once the busy mine shown here, Bessemer is now the haunt of rock collectors.

193

Diamond drillers pause for a photograph at the Helen Mine near Wawa.

their life. A pair of "dinkey" engines were kept busy shunting the ore to the crusher that served both mines. The boarding houses and company store stood about halfway between the two mines. By 1914 the mines were closed and the line removed soon after. Today the mine sites have become popular with rock hounds, while the railway has become a bush trail to the site. Aside from the dumps, only a solitary gravestone in memory of the Childs family lingers along the Bessemer Road south of Highway 28.

Dozens of smaller mines clanged in the bushlands of central Hastings with names like the Sexsmith, the Wallbridge, the Nelson and the Dufferin, and several around Coe Hill. But these would pale compared to what Francis Hector Clergue was about to uncover in a range of mountains that hovered above the northeastern shore of Lake Superior.

Helen Mine

In 1894 Francis Hector Clergue arrived on the shores of Lake Superior with a dream. From the vast resources of the region he envisioned factories, railways and steamships. The realization of that

194

dream began with a piece of rock discovered by prospector Ben Boyer. Clergue recognized it as being iron and went to investigate. In mountains that loomed nearly a thousand feet above a CPR coal dock on Lake Superior, he saw a fortune in iron. He created the mining town of Helen and built a 16-kilometre railway to the lake to haul out its ore. At the mine site he created a self-contained town, complete with a doctor, store, school, and cabins and bunkhouses for the 500 workers and their families. By 1918, however, the ore supply was exhausted and, after producing nearly three million tons of ore, the mine closed.

In 1924 a forest fire swept the area, razing the ghost town along with many buildings in nearby Wawa. But the ghost would not long lay dead. In the 1930s, with the depression claiming victims by the thousands, the Ontario government offered subsidies for the processing of the siderite ore that remained abundant at the mine. The company built a massive sintering plant (which agglomerates ore concentrates for smelting) at Wawa and the Helen roared back to life. Although the Helen closed again in 1962, new open pit operations began nearby, and the great iron range continues to fuel the economy of the area. But the ghosts are never far away.

> **Siderite**
>
> This term is commonly used to refer to the nickel and iron-rich masses found in some meteors. Iron carbonate ($FeCO_3$) is also called siderite or chalybite.

Magpie

In 1909 prospectors named Gibson and Burke discovered another lode of iron about 16 km north of the Helen. A spur line was built to it and the Magpie Mine came to life. Like Helen, it was a self-contained little community. By 1921, however, the demand and price for iron made the mine unprofitable and it closed. Only a few foundations and concrete shells remain at this remote site.

Josephine

Just five kilometres from the Magpie lay another rich deposit of siderite. Here on the shores of Parks Lake, in 1939, the Sheritt Gordon Company opened the Josephine Mine. They added a small townsite and shipped the crushed ore to the sintering plant in Wawa. But the shafts were perilously close to the bottom of the lake and after just six years of production, they collapsed. A couple of other short-lived mines operated in the hills near Wawa. These were the Frances Mine, about 30 km north of Michipicoten Harbour, and the Bartlett Mine, about 33 km east. Of all the ghost mines in the Wawa area, the ruins at the Josephine are the most extensive. Despite vandals' attempts to obliterate them, the headframe, concrete walls, and even a few of the old cabins cling to the steep, rocky shore of the little lake. The only access to it is along the abandoned railway spur.

Sellwood

Sellwood began with the building of the Canadian Northern Railway, and boomed with the opening of the Moose Mountain Iron Mine. By 1909 railway builders William McKenzie and Donald Mann had extended their ambitious railway project north from Toronto to Sudbury. When the Moose Mountain mine began production, about 50 km north of Sudbury, Sellwood became the terminus of the line. Iron was shipped along the railway and onto waiting ships at Key Harbour on Georgian Bay. Although the railway continued on its way northwesterly through Geraldton, Nipigon and Port Arthur, Sellwood continued to thrive as the home for the miners. The townsite contained stores, houses, a pool room, a bake shop, a school, a Chinese restaurant, and the three-story Warren hotel. In 1920 the mine ceased operation (it was restarted in 1957 and from 1963 until the late 1970s shipped iron ore pellets through Depot Harbour) and four years later Sellwood was abandoned. Within 10 years all the buildings had been removed, and the site reverted to forest. Yet in the woods lie a few old foundations of this long-deceased ghost.

THE PLASTER TOWNS

As our kids play with modern play goop like nutty putty, a few of us old-timers may remember creating works of art with plaster of Paris. The Paris in question, however, is not in France, but Ontario. For it was on the banks of the Grand River, a short distance from the town, that William Holmes discovered Ontario's gypsum in 1822. Laid down in ancient seas, the deposit underlies much of Southwestern Ontario (in places as much as 40 feet thick). When exposed, as in riverbanks, it becomes extractable. No fewer than 15 mines began operation along the banks of the Grand following Holmes' discovery.

When they weren't mining gypsum the residents of Mount Healy could be found at choir practice.

Mount Healy

When John Donaldson arrived on the Grand River, the lands were cloaked in thick stands of pine. Here Donaldson built a sawmill and exported lumber down the Grand River canal. In 1838 he built a plaster mill to process the gypsum from the nearby Cook's Mine. It had closed for a while and in 1870 William Donaldson reopened it calling it the Mount Healy Mine. Originally quarried, the four-foot deposit was later extracted through a tunnel. Near the site, on the south shore of the Grand just downstream from the village of York, Donaldson established a townsite. Along a single lane stood a half dozen workers' cabins, while Henry Dochstadter's Mount Healy Hotel served as a boarding house. When the mine closed in 1919, Mount Healy was abandoned — almost. Although the workers' cabins are now little more than depressions in a field, the large and attractive hotel still stands and is now a private home.

Gypsum Mines

On the north bank of the Grand, a short distance south of Cayuga, stood another gypsum "town", called Gypsum Mines. It was the workers' town for such mines as the Excelsior, the Glenny, the Teasdale, and the Merritt. Operated by the Grand River Plaster Company, the town had a grinding mill, a calcinating plant, a handful of cabins and a boarding house. By 1920 the mines had closed, and the little community has since disappeared.

THE CEMENT INDUSTRY

Marl, a fine, white clay found on the bottom of certain lakes, was once essential in the manufacture of cement. Because so much marl was needed, the cement factories found it more economical to locate beside the marly little lakes. Following the turn of the century, cement companies were affected by U.S. tariffs and amalgamations, and most of the lakeside cement towns were abandoned.

Raven Lake

George Laidlaw and William Gooderham are familiar names even today. In 1871 they opened a rail line to the Kawarthas: the Toronto and Nipissing. It never went beyond Coboconk, and remained a marginal line at best dependent on shipments of lumber and farm produce, and loads from large industries at Kirkfield and Raven Lake. One of Ontario's many cement plants, the Raven Lake Portland Cement Company opened here in 1904. The attraction was the deep deposits of marl at the bottom of the tiny lake. Its kilns were capable of producing 700 barrels of cement each day and kept 200 men occupied. In 1914, however, an ill-conceived trade agreement with the U.S. allowed American cement companies to undercut Canadian production so severely that the plant was forced to close. The rails into the complex were lifted and today the roofless, stone ruins of the massive structure lie hidden by the forest. A formidable double chain-link fence beside the railway right of way keeps would-be trespassers sternly at bay.

Kirkfield Quarry

Birthplace of legendary railway builder William McKenzie, Kirkfield remains a prosperous rural village. North of town, the story is different. From the station, still standing about one kilometre north of Highway 48, a spur line branched from the Toronto and Nipissing Railway to the dusty Kirkfield Quarry. Located beside the Trent Canal with its imposing lift lock hovering nearby, the quarry began operation in 1904. The crushers turned out 30 gondola cars of stone each day, while the workers lived in two dozen company houses. When the quarry closed in 1961, the railway's revenue vanished and the line was abandoned. While the pit still yawns behind a chain-link fence, the houses, the machinery and the little dinkey engines were all moved off. The only evidence visible to the public is a wooden freight shed on the old roadbed just north of the Kirkfield station building.

Marlbank

Like Raven lake, the Marlbank operation needed the arrival of a railway to get started. This time it was the Bay of Quinte Railway built from Deseronto to Bannockburn. The plant began operating in 1892 and was enlarged in 1903. About two kilometres east, the railway built their station, and the town of Marlbank appeared. A separate company town was built in the shadow of the cement plant and consisted of several substantial houses and a boarding house. It closed in 1909 when the multinational Canada Portland Cement Company purchased as many as two dozen cement operations and shut them down. Hidden by several decades of forest growth, the stone walls still defy the forces of time, and are the ghosts of Marlbank.

Hybla

This once busy station village on the Central Ontario Railway was the shipping point for the MacDonald Feldspar Mine. The community possessed a boarding house, some private homes, a blacksmith, sawmill, store, and a small shed-sized station. More than 35,000 tons of the gleaming, orange mineral were shipped through Hybla between 1919 and 1929. Today only two of Hybla's original buildings still stand — a house and a former store. A few kilometres away, the mine remains popular with the thousands of rock collectors who annually descend upon the Bancroft area. Hybla lies on the Hybla Road east of Highway 62.

MacDonald Mine

The MacDonald Mine began life in 1919 as the Verona Mining Company with just 10 men. These workers slept at the mine's boarding house or boarded with local farm families, who, with the soil being so poor, welcomed the extra income. In 1929, after shipping

199

Normandale's main street looked a little run down following the closing of Van Norman's iron operation. The hotel (right) despite its dilapidated appearance a hundred years ago, still stands.

more than 35,000 tons of feldspar, the mine closed. The main use of this colourful mineral was historically for making ceramics, electric insulators and artificial teeth. Rock collectors who visit the site are awed at the massive pit they encounter. There are several shafts, one of which is still supported by timber. While some pits are overgrown, others have been freshly worked over, and many samples of the orange rock lie there for the picking. The mine lies on the MacDonald Mine Road, west of the Musclow-Greenview Road.

Black Donald

The orange and blue historic plaque that recounts the story of the Black Donald Graphite Mine seems strangely out of place surrounded by a string of new cottages. But beneath the waters of the lake that sparkles before them are the streets and cellar holes of the 77 buildings that once made up that mining town. Among them were a blacksmith, a Catholic church, a school, recreation hall and three dozen houses. Although the company houses were free, wages were only 10 cents an hour.

Discovered in 1896 by farmer John Moore, the graphite deposit would become the site of one of Canada's largest graphite refineries.

The final product was shipped to Calabogie on the K&P railway and used as an industrial lubricant. While the mine was in production, that lake was in fact a part of the turbulent Madawaska River. The river rapids powered the 400 horsepower generator which provided the village and the refinery with electricity. By the 1950s the deposit began to peter out, and the miners moved away. Ontario Hydro then purchased the ghost town as part of their Mountain Chute hydro power dam. By 1967 the waters behind that dam had flooded most of the site. The new lake was ideal for cottages, and new summer homes were built on the few village streets that managed to stay above the flood line. Now only the plaque and a distant log house (once belonging to a manager) tell the story of this drowned ghost.

Craigmont

Although it is now only a dirt track, the Craigmont Road still earns its own sign. It leads south from the village of Combermere on Highway 62 to the site of what was once Canada's greatest corundum operation. Being one of the world's hardest minerals it was used as an abrasive. There were two townsites, one private, and the other established by the company for a work force that numbered more than 400. Here were houses, bunk houses, and stores, but no tavern. For that the workers had to trudge more than six miles to Combermere.

The gaunt shells of the Cheltenham Brick Works, preserved for the moment, are popular with film crews. "The Wars" was filmed at this location.

201

The mine buildings were dominated by the refinery from which the corundum — in a good year as much as 3,000 tons — was hauled to a landing on the York River, and from there to the railway at Barry's Bay. Production ceased in 1921, after a quarter of a century. Corundum had been replaced by such artificial abrasives as carborundum, and was no longer in demand. The silent fields and woods now contain only the concrete foundations of the old mine buildings.

Cheltenham Brick Works

The massive skeletal shells that lurk beside Mississauga Road north of Terra Cotta look like war-wracked ruins. The Interprovincial Brick Works were built in 1875 three kilometres west of the pretty hamlet of Cheltenham. The massive kilns and chimneys were surrounded by a small workers' village of a dozen or so. In 1958 Domtar purchased the operation and closed it. While the cabins were removed, the looming skeletons of the kilns became a magnet for amateur archaeologists and film crews. Although fenced off, the ruins are saved, for the moment, through an agreement with the brick company that now owns the property.

Forks of the Credit

Now home to wealthy country-dwellers, and popular with fishermen and hikers, it is hard to imagine that the Forks of the Credit was once a busy mining community. From the cliffs of the Niagara Escarpment, which here form a spectacular gorge, miners hacked out massive chunks of building blocks that now sit in such prominent Toronto landmarks as the provincial legislative buildings, Old City Hall, and Casa Loma. To ship the chunks of limestone, the Credit Valley Railway (later taken over by the CPR) added a siding and a spur line. By the mid 1880s, when the quarries operated at their feverish peak, more than 400 quarrymen toiled in three quarries. These included: the Big Hill Quarry near Brimstone, from which huge blocks of limestone were lowered by cable to flatcars on a siding behind the Forks station; the Forks Quarries in the walls that tower above the main canyon; and the Crow's Nest Quarry, a half mile up the Belfountain branch of the railway. A lime kiln near the Forks Quarry and a brick and tile yard across the valley from Brimstone all

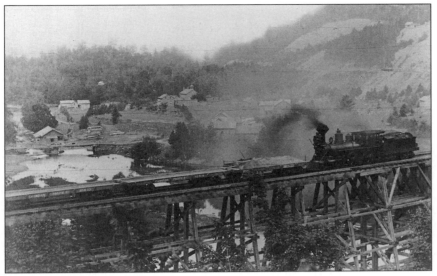

For those who know the area today, this view of the Forks of the Credit may come as a shock. It was snapped when the area had several quarry operations.

made the congested, little valley a busy industrial centre. A pair of miners' villages, Brimstone and Credit Forks, clustered in the bottom of the canyon, while on the rim management and skilled craftsmen enjoyed the breezy luxury of Belfountain.

The rushing river, the forest and the tranquility of the valley today belie that early activity. New buildings began to use concrete instead of quarry stone and by 1920 the little valley was at peace. The Crow's Nest Quarry was closed and absorbed by Charles Mack's luxurious Belfountain estate. That property is now part of the Belfountain Conservation Area; the brickyard has become part of the Caledon Ski Club, while the Forks Quarry and the lime kiln now lie hidden by the forest and visited only by Bruce Trail hikers. Only a few village buildings survived the closing of the mines: at the Credit Forks, a former school and an old house; behind the CPR trestle, the former store; and in Brimstone, a couple of workers' cabins.

In all these vanished and vanishing places, each year the foundations sink a little lower, grass grows up through the railway tracks and moss covers the rubble. These places, and all others like them across Ontario, offer up their silent testimony to the men and women who started with nothing and a dream; and who ended, too often, leaving their dreams behind.

Index

~~~

Recommended Reading

Algoma Eastern Railway, Wilson, Dale
And the Geraldton Way, Lavoie, E.J.
Bell and the Book, Clement, Andrew
Bowering's Guide to Eastern Ontario, Bowering, Ian
Credit Valley Railway, Filby, James
Desperate Venture (Central Ontario Railway), Plomer, J. & Capon, A.R.
Ghosts of the Bay, Chisholm, Barbara ed. (includes Video)
Haliburton by Rail and the IB&O, Wilkins, Taylor
Ignace: A Saga of the Shield, Barr, Elinor and Dyck, Betty
Land of the Big Goose (Wawa and Michipicoten), Turcott, Agnes
Narrow Gauge for Us (Victoria Railway), Cooper, Charles
Northeastern Georgian Bay and Its People, Campbell, William A.
Oliphant and Its Islands, Monckland, Irene
Ontario's First Gold Rush, Eldorado, Boyce, Gerry
Over the Hills to Georgian Bay, Mackay, Niall
Rails to the Lakes (Hamilton and Northwestern Railway), Cooper, Charles
Red Lake Gold Rush, Parrott, D.F.
Silver Centre: The Story of an Ontario Mining Camp, Fancy, Peter

Photo Credits

p. 14	Ontario Archives (ACC 2475 S7673)
p. 23	Metropolitan Toronto Reference Library
p. 30	CP Archives
p. 31	National Archives of Canada
p. 52	Metropolitan Toronto Reference Library (MTL 2052)
p. 76,77	Ontario Ministry of Natural Resources
p. 89	National Archives of Canada
p. 94	Ontario Archives (S 2430)
p. 95	Ontario Archives (ACC 16649-14 F265-2-0-1)
p.101	National Archives of Canada
p.103	Ontario Archives (ACO 14508-3)
p.118	Dave Spaulding
p.120	Ontario Ministry of Natural Resources
p.121	Al Patterson
p.124,125	Ontario Ministry of Natural Resources
p.136	Ontario Bureau of Mines
p.141	Ontario Archives (10456 S16400)
p.142	CP Archives
p.145	National Archives of Canada (10399)
p.147	CN Archives
p.148	Ontario Bureau of Mines
p.150	Ontario Archives (S13660)
p.155	Ontario Bureau of Mines
p.156	Thunder Bay Archives
p.157	Ontario Archives (6907 S13216)
p.166,168	Ontario Ministry of Natural Resources
p.174	Ontario Ministry of Natural Resources (#184)
p.176	Ontario Ministry of Natural Resources (#296)
p.180	Metropolitan Toronto Reference Library
p.186	CP Archives
p.188,193	Ontario Bureau of Mines
p.197,200	Ontario Archives
p.203	Ontario Archives

FRONT COVER: Steamer and Mine Centre Hotel. June 24, 1899
Ontario Archives (ACC 10399-23)
BACK COVER: Stoco Station, Bay of Quinte Railway. circa 1899
Lennox & Addington County Museum (N-3937)
TITLE PAGE: Forks of the Credit. Ontario Archives (ACC 10114-19)

all other photos — Ron Brown